In Memory's Kitchen

In Memory's Kitchen

A Legacy from the Women of Terezín

EDITED BY CARA DE SILVA

TRANSLATED BY BIANCA STEINER BROWN

FOREWORD BY MICHAEL BERENBAUM

ROWMAN & LITTLEFIELD PUBLISHERS, INC.
Lanham • Boulder • New York • Toronto • Oxford

ROWMAN & LITTLEFIELD PUBLISHERS, INC.

Published in the United States of America
by Rowman & Littlefield Publishers, Inc.
A wholly owned subsidary of The Rowman & Littlefield Publishing Group, Inc.
4501 Forbes Boulevard, Suite 200, Lanham, Maryland 20706
www.rowmanlittlefield.com

PO Box 317
Oxford
OX2 9RU, UK

Distributed by National Book Network

The author gratefully acknowledges permission to reprint from the following source:

"An Evening in Terezín" by Eva Schulzová and "I am a Jew and will be a Jew forever"
by Franta Bass from . . . *I never saw another butterfly* . . . , as they appear in te Schocken
Books edition. Copyright © 1993 Schocken Books. Used by permission of the Jewish
Museum in Prague.

First Rowman & Littlefield Publishers, Inc. edition 2006

Copyright © 1996 by Anny Stern, Cara De Silva, and Bianca Steiner Brown

British Library Cataloguing in Publication Information Available

The hardback edition of this book was previously cataloged by the Library of Congress as
follows:

In memory's kitchen: a legacy from the women of Terezín / edited by Cara De Silva ;
 translation by Bianca Steiner Brown and David Stern ; foreword by Michael
 Berenbaum.
  p. cm.
 Includes bibliographical references.
  1. Terezín (Czech Republic : Concentration camp)   2. Cookery, Jewish.   3.
Holocaust, Jewish (1939-1945)   I. De Silva, Cara.
D805.C915   1996
940.53'18'094371—dc20   96-13675
                                                                              CIP
ISBN 1-56821-902-4 (cloth : alk. paper) — ISBN-10: 0-7425-4646-2 (pbk. : alk. paper)
                            ISBN-13: 978-0-7425-4646-2 (pbk. : alk. paper)

Printed in the United States of America

♾™ The paper used in this publication meets the minimum requirements of American
National Standard for Information Sciences—Permanence of Paper for Printed Library
Materials, ANSI/NISO Z39.48-1992.

For Mina Pächter
and
the Women of Terezín

Ten o'clock strikes suddenly,
and the windows of Dresden's barracks darken.
The women have a lot to talk about;
they remember their homes,
and dinners they made.

"An Evening in Terezín" by Eva Schulzová,
from . . . *I never saw another butterfly* . . .

CONTENTS

FOREWORD

Theresienstadt was an anomaly among the German camps. Historians are not quite sure how to describe it; thus, in accounts and memoirs four different terms are used to refer to its diverse functions: garrison city, ghetto, concentration camp, and transit camp. It was the anteroom to Auschwitz for Jews from the Protectorate of Bohemia and Moravia and for special categories of Jews from Germany and Western European countries. These were "prominents," the elderly, and those perceived as having particular merit, often because of distinguished service to Germany during World War I.

But Theresienstadt also had another function. The Nazis artfully positioned it as a model ghetto, a place that purported to demonstrate the Führer's decency to the Jews. However, in reality, it was a means of camouflaging the Reich's actual intentions in order to conceal them from an inquiring world. Behind this Potemkin village, this stage set, Theresienstadt was riddled with fear, disease, and death. This duality, along with the feverish cultural life organized by those interned there, gave the ghetto an almost surrealistic quality.

The origins of Theresienstadt are clear; they can be established with precision. Founded as a garrison town during the reign of Emperor Joseph II in the late eighteenth century, it was named after his mother, the Empress Maria Theresa. On November 24, 1941, Reinhard Heydrich, the head of the SS and *Reichsprotektor* for Bohemia and Moravia, established a Jewish camp in Terezín. Just as Oswiecim became Auschwitz and Lodz became Litsmanschaft, Terezín was called by its German name of Theresienstadt. It was situated conveniently for the function it was to play, just forty miles north of Prague. In November 1941 it became the home of Jews from Prague and then the Jews of the German Protectorate. By July 1942 its non-Jewish population of 7,000 was expelled and the town became a closed Jewish village, with lethal consequences.

Polish ghettos were established shortly after the German invasion of Poland in 1939 and endured until the great deportations of the summer and fall of 1942. In retrospect, they were holding pens, designed to contain the Jews pending a decision on the Final Solution and the creation of the infrastructure—killing centers—that could implement that solution. In contrast, Theresienstadt resembled a transit camp; people were deported to it from Czechoslovakia and the West, and then, beginning shortly after it was established, deported from it to the East. (The "East" was generally a euphemism for the death camp of Birkenau, the section of the Auschwitz concentration camp that served as a killing center, but the destination could also be Treblinka or other camps.)

Conditions in Theresienstadt were harsh. Statistics reveal just how harsh. Some 144,000 Jews were deported to Theresienstadt; of those, 33,000 died there and 88,000 were deported to Auschwitz. By the war's end, only 19,000 were alive. The survival ratio of children was one-half of one percent; 15,000 children were sent to the camp, by the war's end only 100 of them were alive.

In the beginning, the inhabitants of Polish ghettos expected that somehow life would go on. The weight of Jewish history and experience taught that even the worst persecutions ended after a time. The enemy would run out of steam, other concerns would preoccupy them. Hold on for a time, *überstehen*, outlast the enemy—this was a time-honored practice. So the Jews of Poland struggled, valiantly—yet in vain—to carry on a normal life. Most of the Polish ghetto inhabitants were in their own native towns; many remained in their homes.

In contrast, the Jews who were shipped to Theresienstadt were taken from their homes and uprooted from their communities. They, too, imagined, at least for a time, that life would continue, and they, too, struggled courageously—but unsuccessfully—to maintain as normal a life as conditions permitted.

Initially Theresienstadt had been designed for Czech Jews. Soon they were joined by elderly German and Austrian Jews. The term "Austrian Jews" is used with some hesitation. After all, Austria was incorporated into the Reich in 1938 and German and Austrian Jews were homogeneous—linguistically and culturally. Still, the Jews of Vienna thought of themselves as Viennese, just as the Jews of Berlin had thought of themselves as Berliners. Dutch and Danish Jews arrived in the ghetto later.

Some of the older German Jews who came to Theresienstadt were unaware of what was in store for them. They had been told they were eligible for "privileged resettlement," knew the ghetto was in pretty country, had been convinced by German propaganda that it was a spa, and wanted to believe reassurances that they would be treated in a manner appropriate to their stature. As a result, they packed for this journey as they might for any other. According to reliable accounts, some came with top hats and with dresses of proper lace. Some even paid for the privilege of their transport. Upon arrival, they innocently asked for apartments with light, for rooms with a southern exposure.

While they may have come with illusions, the reality of conditions in Theresienstadt confronted them immediately. As many as 53,004 Jews lived in a space that only one year earlier had housed 7,000 Czechs. Food, too, was scarce. In 1942, 15,891 people died, more than half of the average daily population. (In contrast, even in Warsaw the death rate, at its worst, was one in ten.) The death rate was so high at Theresienstadt that a crematorium was built that was capable of handling 190 bodies a day—69,000 a year.

Many prominent Jews came to Theresienstadt. Even under the press of the Final Solution, the Nazis could distinguish between some Jews and other Jews. Status and wealth had its rewards, albeit for just a short time. Some "prominents" had served their country as war heroes during World War I. Army generals might have inquired about their fate. Others had been scientists or industrialists of national and international reputation. Inquiries might have been made regarding their destination. At least for a while, their well-being might have been of interest to someone on the outside. There were also artists and scholars. The Nazis knew that the presence of such talented and skilled people would help perpetuate the hoax of the model ghetto.

Thus, Theresienstadt became the destination and death place of some of the most prominent Czech, Austrian, and German writers, scientists, jurists, diplomats, musicians, professors, and artists. Many of these "prominents" had regarded themselves as citizens of their native lands. Assimilated and acculturated, they had come to regard themselves less as Jews and more as Czechs or Germans. Therefore, their incarceration among Jews, their identification as Jews, came as a shock, a blow to self-esteem.

The density of such talent, the severity of their awful situation, the anxiety about their future gave rise to a rich cultural life surrounded by an all-pervasive sense of death. The cultural life of Theresienstadt was intensified because of the looming sense of mortality.

It is difficult to imagine, yet there was a lending library in Theresienstadt that had tens of thousands of volumes for circulation. Rabbi Leo Baeck, Germany's best-known rabbi, offered courses in philosophy and theology. Yes, Jews spoke of God and to God in the camps.

Symphonic music was written and performed in concert; there was even a children's opera, *Brundibar*. Theatrical performances and lectures gave spiritual sustenance to a dying community. By day, artists in the ghetto workshops painted what was acceptable to their Nazi overseers; at night, they painted a true picture of camp life, hiding their art behind the ghetto walls.

The community was most concerned about its children. Under similar desperate conditions, leaders of Jewish councils throughout Nazi-occupied Europe had different attitudes toward the children, the future of the Jewish people. In Warsaw, Adam Czerniakow tried to protect them. When he could not, he took his own life rather than preside over their deportation. Mordecai Chaim Rumkowski, the head of the Judenrat of Lodz, developed a strategy for survival that sacrificed the children in order to refashion Lodz as a slave labor camp. Thus, in an infamous speech he said: "Brothers, sisters, give me your children." And the children of Lodz were deported to their deaths.

In Theresienstadt the children were educated as if they were middle-class or upper-middle-class Jewish children living under ordinary conditions. They were protected for as long as they could be. A rigorous daily program was developed for them: classes, athletic activities, and art were pursued. Children painted pictures and wrote poetry. Yet because they represented the Jewish future, children were among the earliest to die. They could not be shielded against deportation for long. For example, in August 1943, 1,200 children from Bialystok were deported to Auschwitz. They had spent only one month in Theresienstadt.

Four hundred and fifty-six Danish Jews, many of them elderly and infirm, were sent to Theresienstadt in the fall of 1943. They were the unlucky ones, unable to escape to Sweden during the Danish rescue in October 1943. Yet unlike all other European countries, which quickly lost interest in their deported Jewish citizens, the Danes persisted in their demands for an accounting of their citizens' fate and insisted that the Red Cross visit the ghetto. Elsewhere I have described that visit:

Fearful that any slip of the tongue or crack in the veneer of peaceful village life would further endanger the beleaguered Jews of Theresienstadt, Paul Eppstein, the head of the Jewish Council of Elders (the body that oversaw the ghetto's internal affairs) greeted the guests in black suit and top hat. A band played light music. A cafe created for the occasion was filled with customers. Goods were displayed in store windows. When the delegation came to the soccer field, a goal was scored on cue. Danish Jews, no more than two or three in a room [often rooms had three, four, or many more times that number], were visited in their freshly painted quarters. The children's opera, *Brundibar*, was performed for the guests.

The deception succeeded so well that later a propaganda film was made at Theresienstadt showing how well the Jews were faring under the benevolent protection of the Third Reich. When the filming was over, most of the cast, including the children, was sent to Auschwitz.

In the *chevre kadisha* (the Jewish Burial Society) building in Prague today, one can see the results of the children's activities in Theresienstadt. They can also be seen in the United States Holocaust Memorial Museum and in a deeply touching book appropriate for children—and their parents—entitled . . . *I never saw another butterfly*. . . . The children of Theresienstadt were taught by artist Friedl Dicker Brandeis to express their feelings in drawings. They wrote poetry—words of defiance and of hope. Thirteen-year-old Franta Bass wrote:

> I am a Jew and will be a Jew forever.
> Even if I should die from hunger, never will I submit.
> I will always fight for my people,
> on my honor.

I will never be ashamed of them,
I give my word.

I am proud of my people,
how dignified they are.
Even though I am suppressed,
I will always come back to life.

Hunger was a permanent part of life in the ghetto and the camps. Primo Levi has argued that had the camps lasted but a little longer, a new language would have been required to describe their unprecedented reality.

> We say "hunger," we say "tiredness," "fear," "pain," we say "winter," and they are different things. They are free words, created and used by free men who lived in comfort and suffering in their homes. If the Lagers had lasted longer, a new, harsh language would have been born; and only this language could express what it means to toil the whole day in the wind, with the temperature below freezing, wearing only a shirt, underpants, cloth jacket and trousers, and in one's body nothing but weakness, hunger, and knowledge of the end drawing nearer.

For some, the way to deal with this hunger was to repress the past, to live only in the present, to think only of today, neither of yesterday nor of tomorrow. Not so the women who compiled this cookbook. They talked of the past; they dared to think of food, to dwell on what they were missing—pots and pans, a kitchen, home, family, guests, meals, entertainment. Therefore, this cookbook compiled by women in Theresienstadt, by starving women in Theresienstadt, must be seen as yet another manifestation of defiance, of a spiritual revolt against the harshness of given conditions. It is a flight of the imagination back to an earlier time when food was available, when women had homes and kitchens and could provide a meal for their children. The fantasy must have been painful for the authors. Recalling recipes was an act of discipline that required them to suppress their current hunger and to think of the ordinary world before the camps—and perhaps to dare to dream of a world after the camps.

As such, this work—unlike conventional cookbooks—is not to be savored for its culinary offerings but for the insight it gives us in understanding the extraordinary capacity of the human spirit to transcend its surroundings, to defy dehumanization, and to dream of the past and of the future. One can sense a spiritual toughness in the sisterhood forged in these pages. It adds but another fragment to understanding an event that defies comprehension. For the imagination of those of us who were not there—even of those of us who know the history so well—still cannot approach the inner courtyard of this hell.

Michael Berenbaum, Director
United States Holocaust Research Institute
Washington, D.C.

ACKNOWLEDGMENTS

Many good people have contributed to this act of remembrance in their individual, creative, and practical ways, but none more so than Anny Stern, whose passion to see her mother's book published ceased only with her own death.

Among the host of others to be thanked for their various forms of participation, there are nine who must be specially singled out—Michael Berenbaum of the United States Holocaust Museum, for immediately seeing the importance of the Terezín cookbook and making time for it; Fern Berman, for putting her humanity and talent in the service of this book; Bianca Steiner Brown, for sharing her deep knowledge and having the courage to undertake this painful task; Dalia Carmel, for starting this project down the long road to its present state and standing by it; Jane Dystel of Jane Dystel Literary Management, for her commitment and always wise counsel; Andrea and Warren Grover, for their generosity of spirit and for being there when it mattered most; Wangsheng Li, for appearing out of nowhere to keep it all going; and David Stern, Mina Pächter's grandson, who has been a friend and support. Without their help this book might not have been realized. It is impossible to thank any of them sufficiently.

Others contributed mightily, too. Among them are Dina Abramowicz of YIVO; Barbara Jolson Blumenthal; George Brown; Esther Brumberg of A Living Memorial to the Holocaust-Museum of Jewish Heritage; Susan Cernyak-Spatz of the University of North Carolina at Charlotte; Meira Edelstein of Yad Vashem; Helen Epstein; Rozanne Gold; Carmen Hendershott; Karen Hess; Professor Wilma Iggers; Marion Kaplan of Queens College; David Karp; Professor Barbara Kirshenblatt-Gimblett of New York University; Liesel Laufer; Roland Marandino; Sabina Margulies, Genya Markon of the United States Holocaust Museum; Dr. Jan Munk of Monument Terezín; Joan Nathan; Rabbi Norman Patz; Diana Perez; Alisah Schiller of Beit Terezín and Kibbutz Givat Chaim Ichud; Diane Speilman and Renata Stein of the Leo Baeck Institute; and Václava Suchá of Monument Terezín.

Finally, I would like to express my gratitude to Arthur Kurzweil, Janet Warner, Aliza Stein, and Adam Schindler of Jason Aronson Inc.

Cara De Silva

"Recipes written across a photograph of Hitler": A page from the cookbook written by Malka Zimmet in Lenzing, a branch camp of Mauthausen. A portion of the book was inscribed on multiple copies of a propaganda leaflet for the Third Reich. (Courtesy of Yad Vashem, Jerusalem.)

"Food Delivery": Watercolor and ink on paper. This drawing by Helga Weissová Hosková depicts the food carts that were pulled through the ghetto and was created in Terezín in 1943 when the artist was just 14 years old. Helga and her mother were deported to Auschwitz in 1944, at which time her drawings were given to her uncle, who hid them until liberation. Helga and her mother both survived the war. (Peter Goldberg/Museum of Jewish Heritage.)

"Essenausgabe": Pen-and-ink drawing by Peter Lowenstein. Depiction of aspects of food distribution in the Terezín ghetto—ration cards, wagons laden with barrels of food, and groups of people in food lines. The drawing is an example of the "official" art ordered by the Nazis to show the organization of ghetto life. Lowenstein, a Czech Jew, was deported to Auschwitz in 1944 and perished there. (Peter Goldberg/Museum of Jewish Heritage.)

"Stooping for Potato Peelings": Drawing by Norbert Troller, 1942. Troller (1900–1984) was an architect who was born in Brno. In 1942 he was deported to Terezín where, among other things, he created artworks that depicted the truth of conditions in the camp. In 1944, he was deported to Auschwitz but survived. In 1948, he emigrated to the United States where, ultimately, he opened his own business. The sight of ghetto inhabitants groveling for raw potato peelings was a common one and was depicted by a number of Terezín artists. (Courtesy of the Leo Baeck Institute, New York, and Doris Rauch, Washington, D.C.)

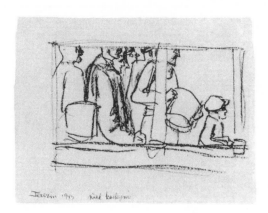

"In Front of the Kitchen": Drawing by Norbert Troller, 1943. The drawing depicts people standing in line to get food. They are clutching the vessels into which it will be ladled. (Courtesy of the Leo Baeck Institute, New York, and Doris Rauch, Washington, D.C.)

"The Sick Room": Watercolor by Norbert Troller, 1942. (Courtesy of the Leo Baeck Institute, New York, and Doris Rauch, Washington, D.C.)

"Mina Pächter in 1939 with her grandson, David Peter Stern": Pächter died in Terezín on Yom Kippur 1944. (Courtesy of David Peter Stern.)

INTRODUCTION

I

No matter how many times Anny told the story, its power to affect her and her listeners never diminished. She was not a person who cried easily; yet even before she began to speak, her lively brown eyes would be brimful of tears.

"I remember so well the day the call came," she would say as she brushed the dampness from her timeworn cheeks, "because it was my past at the other end of the line. 'Is this Anny Stern?' the woman on the phone asked me, and when I answered yes, she said, 'Then I have a package for you from your mother.'"

With those words, a quarter-century-long journey from the Czechoslovak ghetto/ concentration camp of Terezín to an apartment building on Manhattan's East Side came to an end.[1]

Inside the package was a picture taken in 1939 of Anny's mother, Mina Pächter, and Anny's son, Peter (now called David). His arms are around her neck, her beautiful gray hair is swept back, and they are both smiling—but dark circles ring Mina's eyes. There were letters, too—"Every evening I kiss your picture . . . please, Petřičku, do not forget me," Mina had written to her grandson. But it was a fragile, hand-sewn copy book that made up the bulk of the package, its cracked and crumbling pages covered with recipes in a variety of faltering scripts.[2]

---

[1]Terezín is also known as Theresienstadt, its German-Austrian name. Both names will be used interchangeably here.

[2] The history of the Terezín cookbook, as recounted here, is in the form in which Anny Stern told it over the last dozen years of her life. There are several uncertainties in it, but too many people have died to permit resolving them.

Born out of the abyss, it is a document that can be compre-
hended only at the farthest reaches of the mind. Did setting
down recipes bring comfort amid chaos and brutality? Did it
bring hope for a future in which someone might prepare a meal
from them again? We cannot know. But certainly the creation
of such a cookbook was an act of psychological resistance, force-
ful testimony to the power of food to sustain us, not just physi-
cally but spiritually.

Food is who we are in the deepest sense, and not because it is
transformed into blood and bone. Our personal gastronomic
traditions—what we eat, the foods and foodways we associate
with the rituals of childhood, marriage, and parenthood, mo-
ments around the table, celebrations—are critical components
of our identities. To recall them in desperate circumstances is
to reinforce a sense of self and to assist us in our struggle to preserve it. "My mother was already in her seventies at this time,"
said Anny, "yet this book shows that even in adversity her spirit
fought on." And so, too, did the spirits of her friends.

Among their weapons were *Heu und Stroh*, fried noodles
topped with raisins, cinnamon, and vanilla cream; *Leberknödel*,
liver dumplings with a touch of ginger; *Kletzenbrot*, a rich fruit
bread; and *Zenichovy Dort*, or Groom's Cake. There were *Erdäpfel
Dalken*, or potato doughnuts; and *Badener Caramell Bonbons*,
caramels from Baden Baden—about eighty recipes in all. Some
were hallmarks of Central European cookery. A few, like *Billige
Echte Jüdische Bobe*, cheap real Jewish coffee cake, were specifically Jewish. And one, written down by Mina, is particularly
poignant. For *Gefüllte Eier*, stuffed eggs with a variety of gar-
nishes, the recipe instructs the cook to "Let fantasy run free."

"When first I opened the copybook and saw the handwriting
of my mother, I had to close it," said Anny of the day she received the package. "I put it away and only much later did I have
the courage to look. My husband and I, we were afraid of it. It

was something holy. After all those years, it was like her hand was reaching out to me from long ago."

In a way, it was. Just before Mina died in Theresienstadt, she entrusted the package to a friend, Arthur Buxbaum, an antiques dealer, and asked him to get it to her daughter in Palestine. But because most of Anny's letters hadn't reached Mina during the war, she couldn't provide him with an address.

Unable to honor his friend's deathbed wish, Buxbaum simply kept the package. Then one day in 1960, a cousin told him she was leaving for Israel. Still mindful of his promise, he asked her to take the manuscript along, but by the time she got news of Anny and her husband, George Stern, they had moved to the United States to be near their son.

No one knows exactly what happened after that. A letter found in the package and written in 1960 indicates that just as it had been entrusted first to Buxbaum and then to his cousin, so it was entrusted to someone else to carry to New York. Yet according to Anny, it didn't arrive until almost a decade later.

It was then that a stranger from Ohio arrived at a Manhattan gathering of Czechs and asked if anyone there knew the Sterns. "Yes, I have heard of them," responded one woman. A moment later he had produced the parcel and she had become its final custodian. At last, Mina's deathbed gift to her daughter, her startling *kochbuch*, was to be delivered.

Its contents, written in the elliptical style characteristic of European cookery books, are evidence that the inmates of Terezín thought constantly about eating. "Food, memories of it, missing it, craving it, dreaming of it, in short, the obsession with food colours all the Theresienstadt memoirs," writes Ruth Schwertfeger in *Women of Theresienstadt, Voices from a Concentration Camp*.[3]

---

[3]New York: Berg, 1989, p. 38.

Bianca Steiner Brown, the translator of the recipes in this book and herself a former inmate of Terezín, explains it this way: "In order to survive, you had to have an imagination. Fantasies about food were like a fantasy that you have about how the outside is if you are inside. You imagine it not only the way it really is but much stronger than it really is. I was, for instance, a nurse, and I worked at night and I looked out at night—Terezín was a town surrounded by walls, a garrison town. So I looked out at all the beds where the children were, and out of that window I could look into freedom. And you were imagining things, like how it would be to run around in the meadow outside. You knew how it was, but you imagined it even better than it was, and that's how it was with food, also. Talking about it helped you."

Most of us can understand that. Far more disquieting is the idea that people who were undernourished, even starving, not only reminisced about favorite foods but also had discussions, even arguments, about the correct way to prepare dishes they might never be able to eat again.

In fact, such behavior was frequent. Brown remembers women sharing recipes in their bunks late at night. "They would say, 'Do you know such and such a cake?'" she recounts. "'I did it in such and such a way.'"

"The hunger was so enormous that one constantly 'cooked' something that was an unattainable ideal and maybe somehow it was a certain help to survive it all," wrote Jaroslav Budlovsky on a death march from Schwarzheide to Terezín in 1943.[4]

And Susan E. Cernyak-Spatz, professor emeritus at the University of North Carolina and a survivor of Terezín and Auschwitz, describes people in both places as speaking of food

---

[4]The Budlovsky manuscript is in the holdings of Beit Theresienstadt at Kibbutz Givat Chaim—Ichud, Israel.

so much that there was a camp expression for it. "We called it 'cooking with the mouth,' she says. "Everybody did it. And people got very upset if they thought you made a dish the wrong way or had the wrong recipe for it."

It is not far from there to setting down those recipes, and Mina and her friends weren't the only ones to do it.

Two smaller manuscripts (one written entirely in Theresienstadt and one partially written there) are in the possession of Israel's Beit Theresienstadt, the cultural center, library, and archive of Givat Chaim—Ichud, a kibbutz founded by survivors of the ghetto. And there are at least three other recipe collections (one in four parts) and almost certainly more at Israel's Yad Vashem.[5] Undoubtedly, others exist, too.

Of course, paper was a rare commodity in such stark circumstances, and recipes were set down on any kind of scrap available.[6] Take, for example, the four-part manuscript in Yad Vashem. Authored by Malka Zimmet in Lenzing work camp in Austria (Lenzing was a subcamp of Mauthausen), one section is written on multiple copies of a propaganda leaflet telling inmates that those who surround them "Hold the Reich against death and destruction, / stand and fight, a strong stock. / Our promise: Loyalty to the Führer. / Our slogan: Now more so." There are even recipes scrawled around the photograph of Hitler used to illustrate the leaflet.

Unlike Mina's cookbook, which seems to be an accretion of whatever individual contributors felt like setting down, Zimmet's has a classic cookbook format with specific kinds of dishes as-

---

[5]Until now, food has not been a cataloguing category at Yad Vashem, but the holdings are currently being computerized after which it will be easier to find such material.

[6]"If we had had paper at Auschwitz," says Israeli Sabina Margulies, "we would have written recipes down there, too. And if we had been able to write them down we would have had a cookbook of thousands of pages."

signed to each of the four volumes. Writing in Czech and German, she gives recipes for appetizers, desserts, preserves and jams, puddings and fish, meats, vegetables, and specifically Jewish fare. Among the dishes are Karlsbad goulash with sour cream and sauerkraut; a Mikado torte made with caramelized sugar; a dish of carp and potatoes from Serbia; and a matzo brei made with wine and prunes.

Of the other manuscripts, there are Arnoštka Klein's and Jaroslav Budlovsky's, both in Beit Theresienstadt.

Klein writes of sachertorte and a Londoner Schnitten made with marmalade, grated almonds, flour, butter, sugar, eggs, and lemon rind.

Budlovsky, the engineer who began his notes on the death march, wrote recipes down alongside the terse record he kept of the places he and fellow prisoners were forced to walk and of what happened there. "Teichstadt, disappearance of the sick" is the notation for April 23.

He continued his notes after arriving in the ghetto. "This diary was brought to Theresienstadt and is therefore 100% from the time of the camp," he wrote, before he was transported to Auschwitz in December of the same year. Among the dishes he gives recipes for are fladen, small cakes made with goose fat or beef tallow and filled with cheese, ground figs, or chocolate.

While it is likely that, in general, more women than men concerned themselves with recipes in the camps—it was primarily women who cooked at home, after all—there was at least one other World War II cookbook created by men. Published as *Recipes out of Bilibid*, it consisted of recipes by prisoners of war in a Japanese camp in the Philippines. [7]

"Their thoughts were inevitably and ceaselessly focused on

---

[7]New York: George W. Stewart, 1946.

food," wrote Dorothy Wagner in the book's foreword in 1945. "Discussion of its preparation and the heated arguments concerning the superiority of one method over another served as more than an anodyne for their tortured nerves. It strengthened their resolution to survive, if only because it made more vivid, not what they sought to escape from, but what they were resolved to return to."[8]

The same was true in Terezín, of course, because for many the hope of a return to a normal existence was constant. "My life right now is not easy and I suffer everything willingly in the hope of seeing you again," wrote Mina to Anny. But the Terezín cookbook also provided something else.

To a degree that may be unfathomable to Americans at the end of the twentieth century, cooking, both doing it and talking about it, was central to the societies from which many of the women of Terezín, and most European women of the period, came. It was also among the chief activities that defined them as wives and mothers.

Some cooked even in the ghetto, albeit in a limited way. "Theresienstadt really happened after May '42, when all civilians were out and we could move freely and women would try to make some kind of meal while putting rations together," says Cernyak-Spatz.[9]

But a cookbook, even if only imaginatively, offered possibilities for "preparing" foods that were more culturally and psychologically meaningful. While written recipes might not feed the

---

[8]*A Wartime Log*, by Art and Lee Beltrone, a recently published account of prisoner-of-war diaries kept during World War II, also mentions the constant talk of food, the night dreams and daydreams caused by hunger, and the use of log books to write down recipes (Charlottesville, VA: Howell Press, 1995), pp. 122–124.

[9]The Jews were allowed to move freely within the ghetto only after the Czechoslovak townspeople who had occupied Terezín before its complete conversion were gone.

hungers of the body, they might temporarily quell the hungers of the soul.[10]

Possibly, even the book's familiar form brought its authors solace. "It used to be the custom in Europe to make your own written cookbooks," notes Brown. "Probably if I had stayed in Prague and lived the life I left, I would also have started a manuscript cookbook exactly like this one." And the Czech Wilma Iggers, a retired professor of German literature and a Jewish social historian, speaks, too, of the handwritten cookbooks she has from her relatives, from her own Bohemian Jewish background. "It was common," she says. Perhaps the writers of the Terezín cookbook were attempting to preserve this tradition. Perhaps getting the copybook to Anny was important to Mina because it resembled a family manuscript that she might once have given her herself.[11]

But whatever its explicit or implicit functions, Mina's cookbook—and the others—make it clear that half a century after the Holocaust, when we thought we were familiar with all the creative ways in which human beings expressed themselves

---

[10]According to Marion Kaplan in her article "Jewish Women in Nazi Germany: Daily Life, Daily Struggles, 1933–1939," among the many actions the League of Jewish Women took to help its middle-class constituency through the hardships of daily life and the readjustments required by a constantly deteriorating standard of living was to produce a cookbook. "The league," she writes, "knew that people whose social and economic conditions had declined so rapidly needed psychological and material support. One creative way to resist demoralization was to publish a cookbook." Marion Kaplan, *Feminist Studies*, 16:3 (Fall 1990), p. 600.

[11]New York University professor Barbara Kirshenblatt-Gimblett, an expert on the history of Jewish cookbooks, points out that such manuscript cookbooks take many forms, among them the following: Those that transmit gourmet cooking to the Kosher kitchen; those that transmit innovation, not tradition, in the absence of printed cookbooks to do it; those that result from cooking classes, where the students write down the recipes they are taught; and those that are a cook's notations for herself, the result of collecting recipes, exchanging them, copying them from books, clipping newspapers, etc.

during the long years of the horror, at least one small genre, the making of cookbooks, has gone largely unnoticed.

In the case of Mina's manuscript—a product of Terezín, where cultural ferment was constant—such a demonstration of the domestic arts must also be seen as part of a larger artistic whole.

This surrealistic camp, positioned by the Nazis as a model ghetto, evidence of the Reich's benevolence toward the Jews, was the ultimate publicity ploy.[12] Designed to distract the world from the final solution and all that preceded it, it was in fact a way station to the killing centers of the East and itself a place where many died.[13]

Paradoxically, Terezín was also a crucible of creativity. Among the multitude of Central Europeans whom the Reich sent to this "Paradise Ghetto" were painters, writers, musicians, intellectuals, composers, designers, and others who were too well known for their removal to less deceptive places to go unremarked.

Many contrived ways to continue their work—because cultural activities fostered the illusion of a model camp, the Nazis

---

[12]Over the period of its existence, the Nazis conceived of Terezín in a number of different ways—not only as a ghetto with which to dupe the world into believing that Hitler had given a city to the Jews, but, among other things, as a temporary holding pen for the Jews of Bohemia and Moravia and a ghetto for the elderly, though they were transported regularly.

[13]The most dramatic example of this artifice was the "embellishment" undertaken for the inspection visit of the International Red Cross. "There were three or four months of beautification before the Red Cross delegation came," says George Brown, interned in the ghetto at the time. "And a lot of it was pretending there was food. When they came, there was, for instance, a building saying "Dining Hall Number Two," but there had never been a dining hall number one. In fact, there had never been a dining hall at all." George Berkley in his *Story of Theresienstadt* (Boston: Branden Books, 1993), p. 171, recounts the way children were rehearsed for the visit, told to call Karl Rahm, the commandant of the ghetto, Uncle Rahm, and on being given tins of sardines "to exclaim, 'Not sardines again, Uncle Rahm,' as if they had already received too many." For more, see Michael Berenbaum's introduction.

generally turned a blind eye to such endeavors. As a conse-
quence, there flourished in this bizarre environment an artistic
and intellectual life so fierce, so determined, so vibrant, so fer-
tile as to be almost unimaginable.

Despite overcrowding that created pestilent conditions, and
in defiance of raging infections, a high death toll, and hunger—
all as constant a presence as fear of the transports—here the
flower of Central European Jewry participated in what those at
Beit Theresienstadt have called "a revolt of the spirit."

They gave well-attended lectures (Mina Pächter, an art historian, was among the speakers); put on opera performances;
composed music; performed cabaret; drew; painted; and attended
to the education of the young with a fervor born of determination to keep Jewish life alive (and, for some, of determination
to ready the young for a future they hoped they still might have
in Palestine). "It was heroic, superhuman, the care given the
children," says Cernyak-Spatz. "In the face of death, with the
SS looking on, these people tried to persist intellectually and
artistically."

The resulting juxtapositions overwhelm the mind. "Today, the
milk froze in the pot," wrote Gonda Redlich, who kept a diary
throughout his stay in Theresienstadt. "The cold is very danger-
ous. The children don't undress, and so there are a lot of lice in
their quarters. Today, there was a premier performance of *The
Bartered Bride*. It was the finest I had ever seen in the ghetto."[14]

This was what some have described as "the special reality" of
Terezín, and Mina's *kochbuch*, a testament to a lost world and
its flavors, was part of it.

Like most of the cuisines of the Austro-Hungarian empire,
the Czechoslovak kitchen, in which the majority of the writers

---

[14]*The Terezín Diary of Gonda Redlich*, ed. Saul S. Friedman (Lexington: The
University Press of Kentucky, 1992), entry for November 25, 1942, p. 86.

appear to have been raised, placed great emphasis on the plea-
sures of the table. Robust, with sophisticated overtones, it was
well known for its soups; its roast birds and smoked meats; its
savory sausages and wild mushrooms; its moderate use of spices
(caraway and poppy seeds were popular); its goulash and wiener
schnitzel; its large variety of dumplings (eaten from soup to dessert); and its cheeses such as hoop cheese (similar to a dry pot
cheese); yeasted pastries (part of a great baking tradition);
palachinky, sweet crepelike pancakes; and, of course, beer.

Food traditions overlapped with those of Hungary and especially Austria, but also with a number of other countries, the
result of proximity and cultural exchange when all were part
of the Habsburg Empire. Some say it was the Czechoslovaks
who benefited the most; others that it was the other way
around. "Bohemian cooks were held in high regard in Austria.
They were always valued for their skill. The Viennese learned
from us," says Iggers. Of course, Moravian cooks, too, have their
fans.

Regardless of who influenced whom, Czechoslovak cuisine
was beloved, both beyond its natural geographic boundaries and
within them, and eating, at least for the middle class, was a major
pastime.

Listen to author Joseph Wechsberg's impression of Prague. "It
was customary to have five meals a day. Breakfast was at half
past seven in the morning. At ten o'clock, children had their
déjeuner a la fourchette, sandwiches, sausages, hard-boiled eggs,
fruit. Many men would go for half an hour to a beer house for a
goulash or a dish of carved lungs and a glass of beer. Between
ten and ten thirty little work was done in offices and shops;
everybody was out eating. Two hours later, people were having
lunch—at home, since eating lunch in a restaurant was un-
known—and afterward they had a nap. Then to the coffee house
for a demitasse and a game of whist or bridge, and back to the

salt mines for an hour's work" [an exaggeration—most men
worked the afternoon]. Wechsberg also describes the custom of
"a genuine, Central European *jause*, several large cups of coffee
topped with whipped cream, bread and butter, Torte or Guglhopf
. . . and assorted patisserie."[15]

In the countryside or in smaller cities, of course, customs
would have been different, but no less enthusiastic.

What a contrast to the food on which contributors to the
cookbook survived as they wrote their recipes.

Provisions and the means of getting them varied somewhat
over the time of Theresienstadt's existence, but some things
appear to have remained more or less constant. Ask a survivor
about the fare and you are likely to be told of queuing outdoors
for food—often for hours even in inclement weather;[16] of the
daily ration of soup, variously described as tasteless to disgust-
ing; of the sauce that some days might have a tiny bit of meat in
it; of the loaf of bread that had to last three days; of the margarine, the barley,[17] the turnips; and for the fortunate, the food
packages gotten to them by Gentile friends or Jewish organiza-

---

[15]In *Blue Trout & Black Truffles* (New York: Knopf, 1966), p. 14.

[16]In his diary entry for August 11, 1942, Gonda Redlich writes: "The rooms are
full. The people roll about on the floor. They lack utensils. The dead lie among
the living for an entire day, the sick on floors of stone. The walls drip with mois-
ture. At noon, people who live in these houses stand in the courtyards. The food
gets cold. Sometimes it rains." *The Terezín Diary of Gonda Redlich*, ed. Saul S.
Friedman (Lexington: The University Press of Kentucky, 1992), p. 63.

[17]For some, barley became particularly associated with life in Terezín. Shortly
after the ghetto was liberated in May 1945, Gertrud Salomon wrote a poem called
"Barley 1945," in which she compares eating barley in freedom to other foods eaten
by Jews on related occasions. "Barley, Barley is the motto, / Tomorrow we will eat
risotto. / Barley, barley till we burst, / After Pharaoh, Matzoh first. / Soft in coffee,
good for dunking, / And after Haman, hamantaschen. / And now we eat, it tastes
so fine, / Barley after Hitler's time!" From the Elsa Oestreicher Collection in the
Leo Baeck Institute Archives, as cited and translated in the *Leo Baeck Institute News*,
50 (Summer 1985). Reprinted courtesy of the Leo Baeck Institute, New York.

tions on the outside or, earlier on, by family and friends who were still free.

In his memoirs, Norbert Troller, one of the camp's most famous artists, speaks of salads made from weeds;[18] in general no fruits or vegetables were supplied to the population of Theresienstadt.[19]

Cakes were also clever improvisations. Inge Auerbacher, who was a child during her time in the camp, remembers having a palm-sized birthday cake made of mashed potato and a small amount of sugar.[20] And Troller describes a "ghetto torte," saying it was particularly well made by a Mrs. Windholz, whose version "tasted almost exactly like the famous Sachertorte. The recipe was secret;" he writes, "its ingredients . . . bread, coffee, saccharine, a trace of margarine, lots of good wishes, and an electric plate. Very impressive and irresistible."[21]

Though food was sparse and often barely edible, and diseases caused by vitamin deficiencies were a constant problem, to some who went on to Auschwitz, like Chernyak-Spatz or Mina's stepgranddaughter Liesel Laufer, conditions seemed not so bad. The camp's cultural life, described by Laufer as marvelous, also compensated for a great deal.

Others experienced the camp differently. "Like everyone else," Troller wrote, "I suffered greatly from hunger, so that I was plagued all through the day with thoughts of the kind of food I had been used to, as compared to the food we received. Until that time I had hardly ever suffered the pangs of hunger—I could fast for one day during Yom Kippur—but here, without any transition, our

---

[18]In *Theresienstadt, Hitler's Gift to the Jews* (Chapel Hill and London: University of North Carolina Press, 1991), p. 77.

[19]In his diary entry for May 5, 1943, Gonda Redlich, op cit., p. 116, mentions a young girl who is sent to prison for five weeks for stealing a head of lettuce.

[20]*I Am A Star, Child of the Holocaust* (New York: Puffin Books, 1993), p. 48.

[21]Troller, op. cit., pp. 120–21.

rations were shortened to such an extent (approximately one-third of the customary calories in their most unappetizing form) that hunger weakened and absorbed (one's) every thought."[22]

But while almost all were hungry, some were more hungry than others. In the early days of Theresienstadt (May 1942), it had become clear to the Council of Jewish Elders, the group forced by the Nazis to run the internal affairs of the camp, that the limited food supplies could not be divided equally. They determined that those who labored at the hardest jobs had to be allotted more to eat than those whose work was less arduous and that children, the hope of the future, also had to be fed more than others.

They decided, too, that the fewest calories—and usually the worst accommodations—would have to go to those least likely to survive the ordeal of Terezín, namely, the elderly like Mina Pächter, who had been born in 1872 and was 70 when she arrived in the ghetto. Such people were sacrificed so others might live. "For younger people, Theresienstadt was bearable," says Liesel Laufer. "For older people, it was hell."

One must suppose that Mina passed many sorrowful nights remembering that despite her daughter's entreaties, she had refused to accompany Anny when she left for Palestine late in 1939.

After spending nine months struggling to expedite the emigration of Jews at the Prague Palestine Office[23] under Adolf Eichmann and his staff,[24] it had become increasingly clear to Anny that she and her son now had to leave themselves (her husband was already in Palestine). She pleaded with her mother

---

[22]Ibid., pp. 94–95.

[23]The Reich set up a number of Palestine offices to facilitate emigration, a somewhat more benign method of getting rid of Jews than the methods that were to follow. Many Jews were eager to go, but few countries would accept them, which caused a massive bottleneck.

[24]Anny recounts a meeting with Eichmann during which he asked, "Are you a Zionist?" When she answered, "Jawohl," he replied, "Good, I am a Zionist, too. I want every Jew to leave for Palestine."

to come, too, but Mina replied, "You don't move an old tree. Besides, who will do anything to old people?"

She was shortly and tragically to find out who.

How one fared in Theresienstadt depended to a certain extent on how well one could negotiate the system. Norbert Troller, for instance, traded portraits of the cooks and bakers to their subjects for extra food; others schemed to get jobs that permitted them greater access to provisions. But the elderly, writes Zdenek Lederer in *Ghetto Theresienstadt,* "unlike the young workers had no access to the food stores of the Ghetto, while their debility prevented them from making clandestine contacts with a view to acquiring some food.

"Starving elderly men and women begged for watery soup made from synthetic lentil or pea powder, and dug for food in the garbage heaps rotting in the courtyard of the barracks," he writes. "In the morning, at noon, and before nightfall they patiently queued up for their food clutching saucepans, mugs or tins. They were glad to get a few gulps of hot coffee substitute and greedily ate their scanty meals. Then they continued their aimless pilgrimage, dragging along their emaciated bodies, their hands trembling and their clothes soiled."[25]

"The decision [to reduce their rations] transformed many of the elderly into scavengers and beggars," writes George Berkley in *The Story of Theresienstadt.*[26] "They would . . . pounce on any morsel of food such as a pile of potato skins, food considered fit only for pigs." (This scene was so common that it is frequently depicted by Terezín artists). As a result of eating the raw peelings, many of the elderly developed severe enteritis and diarrhea, a chronic camp condition but especially common, and especially serious, among the aged.

---

[25]New York: Howard Fertig, 1983, pp. 48–49.
[26]Boston: Branden Books, 1993, p. 55.

No one knows for certain to what degree this describes Mina's life in Theresienstadt, but we do know it was extremely hard. (Her family believes she escaped transportation only because she had been given an order of merit from the German Red Cross for her aid to German soldiers passing through Czechoslovakia during World War I.)

By the time she was found in the fall of 1943 by her step-granddaughter Liesel Laufer, who had been sent to Terezín earlier that year, Mina was suffering from protein deficiency, a condition referred to as hunger edema. "An acquaintance of my parents told me where she was, and she was in living quarters that were very bad," says Liesel, now a resident of Israel. "When I came, she was really in a poor state. She was suffering very badly from malnutrition. And I saw that she couldn't take care of herself anymore."

Because she was a nurse, Liesel was able to get Mina into the hospital, where she was able to look after her a little. Hospitalization also meant that Liesel's husband, Ernest Reich, a doctor, could include Mina in his study of the effects of protein deficiency. Along with other patients, she was allotted two spoonfuls of white cheese a day (all that was available) to see what effect that small addition to her regular diet would have on her health. It was of little use.

Mina's fear, expressed in one of her poems, that no good would come to her in Terezín proved warrented. She never got to kiss her grandson again. On Yom Kippur 1944, she died in the ghetto hospital.

II

Though written in recipes, the collective memoir that Mina and her friends left behind is in some ways as revealing as prose. It may not impart biographical details, but if we didn't already know the condition its authors were in and the circumstances under which their cookbook had been created, we could still discern their distress from the recipes. They, too, bear witness.

Whether because of illness or disorientation, an unsettling interruption, or the discovery that a contributor's name was on a transport list, a number of the recipes are muddled or incomplete. In some an ingredient is left out (the bean torte, for instance, usually requires an egg; the cream strudel has no dough); in others a process is omitted (dumplings are made and sauced without ever being cooked). Steps are inverted, and punctuation, too, is often nonexistent or perplexing.

The recipes also reflect the fact that it was wartime. One is actually entitled *Kriegs Mehlspeise*, or War Dessert; one, *Tobosch Torte*, calls for imitation honey, several others for coffee substitute, and many for margarine, which almost certainly would have been butter in peacetime, when it was less scarce. Eggs were rationed and often appear in parentheses indicating that one should be used if you have it, but that such use is optional.[27]

We can also tell, because not all the recipes are Kosher, that for the most part they were likely to have been written by Jews from Bohemia and Moravia. Czechoslovakia certainly had Orthodox and observant Jews—"The religious split in town ran straight through the populace's Sunday menu: the Jews had Wiener Schnitzel, the Gentiles had roast pork with sauerkraut

---

[27]Actual shortages were probably much more acute than this, however. And they were particularly acute for Jews. "Even before deportations began," writes Karel Lagus in *Terezín*, "the Jews were already being systematically starved under wartime rationing. Their ration books were stamped 'J.' On such rations books no white bread, meat, eggs, were issued. Jews were not allowed to receive any pulse, fruit, jam and marmalade, stewed fruit, cheese, and other dairy products, sweets, fish and fish products, poultry and game, yeast, sauerkraut, onions and garlic, honey, alcoholic drinks including beer, etc." (Prague: Council of Jewish Communities in the Czech Lands, 1965), p. 16.

and dumplings," wrote Joseph Wechsberg in *Blue Trout & Black Truffles*.[28] But Bohemian Jews in general were among the most assimilated in Europe. For many, this meant that Jewishness was maintained through tradition, community, and perhaps holiday *shul*-going rather than through *kashruth*.[29]

Readers of German will notice, too, that the original language of the recipes (only occasionally were they written in Czech) is sometimes ungrammatical, rough-hewn, Slavicized, or misspelled. Much of this may have resulted from disabling weakness, chemical imbalances caused by malnutrition, or fear, but it is likely there were also other causes. For some of the writers, for example, German may have been a second, imperfectly mastered language, one they spoke but didn't write. (Bianca Steiner Brown points out that while the recipe for cheesecake makes bumpy reading in German, it would be phrased perfectly if its author, probably a native Czech speaker, had been writing in Czech.)

In these ways Mina's haunting cookbook reveals its sad genesis. To alter the recipes would be to violate history and to misrepresent the experiences of the women who produced them. Translations, therefore, have been kept as literal as possible, grammatical errors have been retained, and although recipes have been clarified where necessary (clarifications always appear in brackets), they have not been corrected. Likewise, the measurements used have been left intact—it would be inappropriate to replace the culinary signposts of the writers' culture with our own—but equivalents are given in the section of this book

---

[28]Op. cit., p. 14.

[29]According to Helen Epstein, author of *Children of the Holocaust*, this resulted from the fact that "at the end of 18th century, the Habsburg Emperor Joseph the Second, basically ordered Jews to go to German schools and give up Jewish culture for German culture, and the Jews to the East rejected this and the Bohemian and to a lesser degree the Moravian Jews, smaller and more dispersed, accepted it."

titled Practical Notes. The only changes are in the English version, where alterations have sometimes been made in punctuation, and grammar has sometimes been corrected, or a sentence has been broken up to facilitate the reading of recipes that would otherwise have been too difficult to follow.

Listen as you turn the pages and you will occasionally hear their authors' voices rising above the pit. *"Sehr gut"*—"Very good"—writes one contributor of her cake. *"Lasse der Fantasie freien Lauf"*—"Let fantasy run free"—says Mina in her *Gefüllte Eier*. They are precious sounds.

"The farther away it is, the worse it seems, this enormous thing that happened to the Jews," said Anny late one afternoon as she clutched the cookbook in her elegant hands. "When you look in the caldron, you can't believe what was in it. Yet here is the story of how the inmates of the camp, living on bread and watery soup and dreaming of the cooking habits of the past, found some consolation in the hope that they might be able to use them again in the future. By sharing these recipes, I am honoring the thoughts of my mother and the others that somewhere and somehow, there must be a better world to live in."

Cara De Silva
New York City

Kochbuch

Vally Grabscheid

Mina's
Cookbook

Recipes

Mürber Strudel

20 dkg Mehl, 10 dkg Kartoffelmehl, 10 dkg Zucker, 12 dkg Sana, (1 Ei), Soda od. Backpulver. Wie Strudel beliebig füllen.

Flaky Strudel

20 decagrams flour, 10 decagrams potato flour, 10 decagrams sugar, 12 decagrams Sana [margarine], (1 egg), baking soda or baking powder. Like strudel, fill as desired.

—◄►—

Ženichový Dort

2 Eiweiß mit 16 dkg Zucker ½ Stunde rühren, 6 Eiweiß Schnee, 16 dkg Zucker, 24 dkg Schokolade aufkochen mit 6 Eßl. Wasser zu gerührten Eiweiß verrühren zum Schluß den Schnee. Bei offener Röhre backen.

Groom's Cake

2 egg whites with 16 decagrams sugar. Stir for ½ hour. 6 egg whites [stiffly beaten to] snow. Bring to a boil 16 decagrams sugar, 24 decagrams chocolate with 6 tablespoons water. Add to the stirred egg whites. At the end add the snow. Bake with oven door slightly ajar.

Bohnen Torte

30–35 dkg gekochte Bohnen mahlen, 10 dkg Zucker mit 2 dkg Marg. rühren, die Bohnen dazugeben, etwas Backpulver, bißchen Milch, etwas Grieß od. Mehl. In einer gut beschmierten Form backen.

Bean Cake

Grind 30–35 decagrams boiled beans. Stir 10 decagrams sugar with 2 decagrams marg. [margarine], add beans, some baking powder, a little milk, some farina or flour. Bake in a well-greased [cake] pan.

Tobosch Torte (Fr. Beran)

16 dkg Zucker, 2 Eßl. Kunsthonig, 6 dkg Sana, 4–6 Eßl. Milch, 1 Ei, am Feuer sprudeln bis es kocht. Wenn ausgekühlt, einen Kaffeelöffel Speisesoda dazu geben. Am Brett mit 40 dkg Mehl verarbeiten; 4–5 grosse Blätter backen. Gute Kaffeecreme machen.

Tobosch Torte (Mrs. Beran)

16 decagrams sugar, 2 tablespoons artificial honey, 6 decagrams Sana [margarine], 4–6 tablespoons milk, 1 egg. Stir over fire until it boils. When cooled add 1 coffeespoon baking soda. On a board, work in 40 decagrams flour. Bake 4–5 large layers. Make a good coffee cream [frosting].

Makaronen

2 Tassen Haferflocken, 2 Tassen Mehl, 1 Tasse Zucker, 2–3 dkg Sana, bisschen Milch, Backpulver oder Soda, (1 Ei) Kugeln formen, in die Mitte eine Vertiefung u. Marmelade.

Macaroons

2 cups rolled oats, 2 cups flour, 1 cup sugar, 2–3 decagrams Sana [margarine], a little milk, baking powder or [baking] soda. (1 egg.) Form into balls. In the middle [put] an indentation and jam.

⊷ ⊨◆⊨ ⊶

Linzer Torte

20 Löffel Mehl, 8 Löffel Zucker, 4 Löffel Essig, 2 Eier, 10 dkg Margarine, 1 Backpulver, etwas Milch. Beliebig füllen.

Linzer Torte

20 spoons flour, 8 spoons sugar, 4 spoons vinegar, 2 eggs, 10 decagrams margarine, 1 [packet] baking powder, some milk. Fill to your liking.

⊷ ⊨◆⊨ ⊶

Butter Kindeln

*16 dkg Butter, 16 dkg Mehl, 2 Dotter, 2 Löffel Essig, etwas Salz, 1
Kaffelöffel Zucker, den Teig rasten lassen.
Fülle: 10 dkg Nüsse, 10 dkg Zucker, ½ Zitrone S. & Sch.,
½ Orange, Zimt.*

Butter Kindeln

16 decagrams butter, 16 decagrams flour, 2 egg yolks, 2 spoons
vinegar, some salt, 1 coffeespoon sugar. Let dough rest.
Filling: 10 decagrams nuts, 10 decagrams sugar, ½ lemon, juice
& rind, ½ orange [juice and rind], cinnamon.

[Czech Cake 1]

25 dg hladké mouky, 8 dg tuku, 8 dg cukru, 1 vejce, 3 lžice mléka, ½ prášku, plnit podle chuti.

25 decagrams [smooth] flour [similar in texture to our all-purpose flour], 8 decagrams fat [margarine], 8 decagrams sugar, 1 egg, 3 spoons milk, ½ [packet] baking powder. Fill to taste.

[Czech Cake 2]

25 dg mouky, 15 dg vařených lisovaných brambor, 10 dg tuku, 10 dg cukru, 1 vejce, 2 lžice mléka, prášek, plnit.

25 decagrams flour, 15 decagrams boiled pressed potatoes [put through a potato ricer], 10 decagrams fat [margarine], 10 decagrams sugar, 1 egg, 2 spoons milk, baking powder, fill.

Griess Knödel

½ kg Griess, 1 Löffel Fat gebe in Wasser, bisl Salz, und brühe den Griess ab, treibe es gut ab u. lasse es auskühlen. Dann gebe dazu 3 Dotter u. 3 Eiweiss Schnee. Mache daraus Knödel, wenn selbe zum Fleisch sind, so werden selbe 2–3 Minuten gekocht, nicht länger gekocht. Sind selbe als Mehlspeis so kommt Zucker dazu entweder im Wasser gekocht oder im Fett schwimmend ausgebacken und mit Zucker und Zimt bestreuen.

Farina Dumplings

Put ½ kilogram farina, 1 spoon fat [with] a little salt in water, and scald the farina. Mix it well and let it cool. Then add 3 egg yolks and 3 egg whites [stiffly beaten to] snow. Make dumplings out of it. If same are with meat, boil them not longer than 2–3 minutes. If same are for dessert, sugar is added. [Dumplings are] either boiled in water or fried swimming in fat and sprinkled with sugar and cinnamon.

Kirsch–Zwetschken Knödel

5 dkg Butter, 10 dkg passierten Topfen, ⅛ 1 Milch gew. Semmel, 1 Ei, 1 Kaffeelöffel Salz, 15 dkg gek. passierte Kartoffel, 30–40 dkg gr.Mehl; gut durcharbeitet. Ca 56 Knödel schneiden, formen, in Salzwasser 6–8 Minuten kochen.

Cherry–Plum Dumplings

5 decagrams butter, 10 decagrams Topfen [curd] passed through a sieve, 1 roll soaked in ⅛ liter milk, 1 egg, 1 coffeespoon salt, 15 decagrams boiled potatoes passed [through a potato ricer], 30–40 decagrams coarse flour [the texture of farina]; well-worked. Cut about 56 dumplings, form them, and boil in salted water 6–8 minutes.

Ausgiebige Schokolade Torte

10 dkg Butter, 10 dkg Zucker, 4 Dotter, 14 dkg erweichte Schokol. abtreiben; 4 Schnee, 3 dkg Mehl. Eine dünne Platte in einer Tortenform backen, den Rest am Blech und zerbröseln. In der Form immer eine Lage Creme, 1 Lage Brösel obenauf Glasur, oder Sahne. Creme: 14 dkg Schok. m. 5 dkg Zucker, 2 Löffel Wasser am Feuer verrühren, ½ l Schlagsahne hinein.

Rich Chocolate Cake

Beat 10 decagrams butter, 10 decagrams sugar, 4 egg yolks, 14 decagrams softened chocolate. Fold in 4 [egg whites stiffly beaten to] snow, 3 decagrams flour. Bake a thin layer in a cake pan. [Pour] the rest [of the batter] on a baking sheet, [bake] and make crumbs [from it]. In cake pan always put a layer [of] cream, a layer [of] crumbs. Top with glaze or cream. Cream: 14 decagrams choc. with 5 decagrams sugar, 2 spoons water. Mix over fire. Fold in ½ liter whipped heavy cream.

Leberknödel

Weiche 4–5 Semmeln ein, Jetzt zerschneide
½ Kg Kalbsleber oder noch besser Gansleber,
+ dünste sie ein, nur auf Zwiebel +
fett ab, Jetzt zerwiege die Leber mit
dem Hackmesser ganz fein gebe sie
in die abgetriebenen geweichten Semmel
Gebe dann einen grossen Löffel Gansfett
5 Dotter Pfeffer + Ingwer von den
Eiweiss mache Schnee, man kann es auch
die Eier ganz geben, gebe dann etwas
Petersilie 20 Deca Semmelbrösel + 20 Deca
Mehl, forme daraus Knödel + obenauf
werden sie mit Zwiebel + Semmelbrösel
bestreut. Man gibt dann in Fett Rothkraut
oder Kraut von Kohlrabi. Nicht zerschneide,
im Ganzen servieren.

Apfel Knödel

Mache einen ganz gewöhnlichen Knödelteig
mit ½ Kg Mehl 2 Eier ½ Deca Hefe, Jetzt zerschneide feine zarte Apfel auf kl. Stücke gleich
müssen selbe vor dem Schwarzwerden bewahrt
werden indem man sie mit ein Weinwein
begiesst, wenn der Teig durchgearbeitet ist
gebe die Apfel hinein + mache gewöhnliche

Leberknödel

Weiche 4–5 Semmel ein. Jetzt zerschneide ½ kg Kalbsleber oder noch besser Gansleber & dünste auf Zwiebel und Fett ab. Jetzt zerwiege die Leber mit dem Hackmesser ganz fein. Gebe sie in die abgetriebenen geweichten Semmeln gebe dazu einen grossen Löffel Gansfett, 5 Dotter, Salz & Pfeffer & Ingwer von den Eiweiss Schnee; man kann auch die Eier ganz geben, gebe dazu etwas Petersilie, 20 Deca Semmelbrösel & 20 Deca Mehl, forme daraus Knödel. Obenauf Zwiebel in Fett, Semmelbrösel bestreuen. Dazu Rotkraut oder Kohlrabi Kraut. Nicht zerschneiden, im Ganzen servieren.

Liver Dumplings

Soak 4–5 rolls. Now cut ½ kilogram calves liver, or, even better, goose liver and stew on onion and fat. Now mince the liver with a chopping knife. Add to the softened mashed rolls. Add 1 large spoon goose fat, 5 egg yolks, salt & pepper & ginger and from [stiffly beaten] egg whites snow. One can also add whole eggs. Add a little parsley, 20 decagrams breadcrumbs & 20 decagrams flour. Form into dumplings. [The boiling of the dumplings is omitted.] Top with onion [sautéed] in fat [and] sprinkle breadcrumbs. Accompany with red cabbage or kohlrabi cabbage. Do not cut [dumplings], serve them whole.

·—·◄◆►·—·

Apfel Knödel

*Mache einen ganz gewöhnlichen Knödelteig mit ½ kg Mehl, 2 Eier,
½ Deca Hefe, etwas Fett. Jetzt zerschneide feine zarte Äpfel auf kl.
Stücke gleich müssen selbe vor dem Schwarzwerden bewahrt werden,
indem man sie mit bisl Weisswein begiesst; wenn der Teig durchgearbeitet ist gebe die Äpfel hinein und mache gewöhnliche Knödel.
Reiche dazu Zwetschken Röster. Ist ein gutes Abendbrot.*

Apple Dumpling

Make an ordinary dumpling dough with ½ kilogram flour, 2 eggs,
½ decagram yeast, some fat. Now cut fine delicate apples into
small pieces. To prevent them from darkening, pour some white
wine over apples. When the dough is kneaded, add apples and
make ordinary dumplings. Serve with stewed prunes. It is a good
supper.

Kartoffel Salat

*½ kg Kipfel Kartoffel mit Schale kochen, schälen, schneiden. Mit 1
kl. Schöpfer kochender Suppe oder Wasser begiessen. Öl dazugeben,
dann erst Essig, Salz, Pfeffer, Zwiebel, (Äpfel, Herring, Gurke).
Falls mit Mayonnaise, die heiß darüber giessen.*

Potato Salad

Boil ½ kilogram Kipfel potatoes [small horn-shaped potatoes]
in their jackets. Peel and cut. Pour over 1 small ladle boiling
broth or water. Add oil, then vinegar, salt, pepper, onion (apples,
herring, cucumber [pickles]). If mayonnaise [is used], pour it over
hot.

――― ≖◆≖ ――

Hirse Knödel

*20 dkg Hirse brühen im Wasser dick einkochen mit 2 Löffel Zucker,
etwas Salz. Am nächsten Tag mit 5 dg Kartoffelmehl und 1 Ei
verrühren und mit nassen Händen Knödel formen und mit Marmelade füllen. (16 Stück)*

Millet Dumplings

Scald 20 decagrams millet in water with 2 spoons sugar, some
salt and boil until thick. The next day, mix with 5 decagrams
potato flour and 1 egg. With wet hands, form dumplings and fill
them with jam. (16 pieces)

――― ≖◆≖ ――

Feine Palfy Knödel

Zerschneide in Würfel 10 Semmeln, gebe in eine Schüssel, dazu viel gewiegte Petersilie. Begiesse mit 15 dkg Butter, jetzt zerquirle 5 ganze Eier mit 5–6 Löffel Milch; giesse über die Semmeln. Lasse ½ Stunde stehen, gebe dann 5–6 Löffel Mehl dazu, nur dass es gut zusammen hält; forme Orangen grosse Knödel und koche selbe 15–20 Minuten zerschneide sie u. gib sie zu Tisch. Das Verhältnis ist ung. per Person 2 Semmel und 1 Ei.

Delicate Palfy Dumplings

Cut 10 rolls into cubes. Place them in a bowl, add a lot of chopped parsley and pour over 15 decagrams melted butter. Now whisk 5 eggs with 5–6 spoons milk. Pour over rolls and let stand for ½ hour. Add 5–6 spoons flour, just enough to hold the dough together. Form large dumplings, the size of an orange, and boil them for 15 to 20 minutes. Cut them and bring them to the table. The proportion is approximately 2 rolls and 1 egg per person.

Ganshals mit Griess gefüllt

Der Ganshals wird auf der schmalen Seite zugenäht mit folg. farce gefüllt. 10–15 dkg Griess, ½ fein geschnittene Semmel, Salz, Pfeffer, Ing. das Ganze mit 2–3 Löffel kochendem Fett gebrüht mit heisser G. Suppe zu einem Brei vermengt, und gefüllt. Der Hals zugenäht, in der Suppe 25 Min. gekocht dann auf Fett gebraten.

Goose Neck Stuffed with Farina

Sew the small side of the gooseneck [skin] together and fill it with the following farce: 10–15 decagrams farina, ½ fine-cut roll, salt, pepper, ginger. Scald [mixture] with 2–3 spoons boiling fat and enough hot goose broth to form farce. Stuff [the gooseneck]. Sew the neck together. Boil it in the [goose] broth 25 minutes, then roast on fat.

Zwiebel Kuchen

Mache einen mürben Teig oder Blätterteig, belege ganz dünn auf ein gefettetes Blech. Jetzt dünste ungef. 10 Zwiebel in 15 dkg Fett; die dürfen nicht brown werden. Dazu 1 Löffel gestossenen Kümmel, eine Prise Salz, 2–3 Stückchen Zucker; gebe dazu 3 Löffel Mehl und stelle es weg, wenn es kalt ist, gebe dazu 3 Dotter, 1 Glas dicken sauren Schmetten, und den Schnee. Streiche dies auf die Teigplatte und backe es in mässig heisser Röhre, und zerschneide kleine Carros daraus.

Onion Kuchen

Make a flaky dough or puff pastry. Lay it very thinly on a greased baking sheet. Now stew about 10 [sliced] onions in 15 decagrams fat without browning them. Add 1 spoon pounded caraway seeds, a pinch of salt, 2–3 pieces of sugar [tablets]. Add 3 spoons flour and set aside. When cool, add 3 egg yolks, 1 glass thick sour cream and [egg whites, stiffly beaten to] snow. Spread this on the dough layer and bake it in a medium hot oven and cut into small squares.

Winter-Salat

2 grosse Krautköpfe, 2 kg Zwiebel, 2 kg grüne Paradeiser, 11 grüne Paprikaschoten, schneidet man nudelig und vermengt es mit 40 dkg Salz. In einem Sack lässt man das über Nacht hängen und abtropfen. Dann drückt man das Gemüse aus, gibt es in eine Schüssel und begiesst es mit 3 Liter kochendem Essig. Nach 6 Stunden wird der Essig abgegossen und das ausgedrückte Gemüse mit 6 Esslöffel Senfkörnern and 1 Esslöffel gestossenem Neugewürz vermengt. Den Essig hat man inzwischen mit ½ Liter Wasser u. ½ kg Zucker abgekocht u. ausgekühlt mit dem Gemüse vermengt. Füll es in Gläser, verbinde sie u. nach 1 Monat ist der Salat gebrauchsfähig. Er hält 3 Jahre.

Winter Salad

2 large cabbage heads, 2 kilograms onion, 2 kilograms green tomatoes, 11 green peppers cut into thin strips. Mix with 40 decagrams salt. Pour vegetables into a sack and let it hang overnight and drain. Then squeeze the vegetables, put them into a bowl and pour 3 liters boiling vinegar [over them]. After 6 hours strain the vinegar and squeeze vegetables. Mix them with 6 tablespoons mustard seeds and 1 tablespoon pounded allspice. In the meantime, the vinegar has been boiled with ½ liter water and ½ kilogram sugar, and [when] cooled [is] mixed with vegetables. Put into jars. Cover and tie them and let them stand. Can be used after 1 month. Salad will keep for 3 years.

———— ✠ ————

Billige echt jüdische Bobe

Mache einen gewöhnlichen lockeren Hefeteig, wenn es aufgegangen ist, gebe den Teig aufs Nudelbrett. Walke ihn aus, reibe darauf einige Kartoffeln, viel Zucker und Zimt und kaltes Gänsefett, ungef. 2–3 grosse Löffel. Blättere dies genau 3 Mal walke den Teig, gebe ihn in die Pfanne, gebe darauf halb Powidl und halb eine gute Mohnfülle. Gebe den Teigdeckel fest darauf, bestreiche es mit Fett und backe es in mittelheisser Röhre.

Cheap Real Jewish Bobe [Coffee Cake]

Make a plain loose yeast dough. When it is risen, place dough on a noodle board. Roll it out. Grate several potatoes onto dough, sprinkle with a lot of sugar and cinnamon, about 2–3 large spoons cold goose fat. Fold and roll dough exactly 3 times. Put [half] in [cake] pan. Top it half with prune butter and half with a good poppy seed filling. Top tightly with dough cover. Spread it with fat and bake it in a medium hot oven.

Billige Hagebutt Pusserln

4–5 Eiweiss Schnee gebe dazu 20 D Zucker und 15 D Haselnüsse dies schlage im Wasserbad bis es dick und warm ist; gebe dazu 4–5 Löffel Hagebutt Marmelade und 3–4 Löffel Stärke od. Kartoffelmehl. Mache mit dem kl.Löffel auf Oblaten Pusserln und backe es in lauer Röhre.

Cheap Rose Hip Kisses

[To] 4–5 [egg whites stiffly beaten to] snow, add 20 decagrams sugar and 15 decagrams hazelnuts. Beat in waterbath until thick and warm. Add 4–5 spoons rose hip jam and 3–4 spoons cornstarch or potato starch. With the small spoon make kisses on oblaten [small rounds of edible wafer] paper and bake in a low oven.

Schüssel Pastete

Mache einen Blätterteig den man 3–4 Mal geblättert hat, gebe ein ausgewalktes Stück von dem Teig in die Form wo Du es auf den Tisch gibst, backe dies halb in heisser Röhre. Jetzt mache einen grossen Papierbausch auf die Pastete mache rings herum aus dem Teig einen Rand und einen Teigdeckel lege auf den mit Fett bestrichenen Papierbausch bestreiche den mit Ei und backe es in heisser Röhre.
Unterdessen mache Dir die Pastenfülle vorbereitet und z[war] entweder junges Gemüse od. Hirn mit Ei od. Schwämme mit Ei oder eine richtige Farce gebratenes Kalbfleisch und Hühnerfleisch, wird fein gehackt, 1 Kalbshirn gebraten, 15 Dkg Zunge, od. Selchfleisch, 3 Sardellen, 3 geweichten Semeln, 3 ganze Eier, Schwämme, Hahnenkämmchen ein dicker Bechamell, zitronensaft, ½ Glass Weisswein, Pastetengewürz; schmecke es ab und gebe es in die Form. Den Deckl hebe vorsichtig ab, gebe den Papierbausch weg und gebe diese farce so heiss als möglich in die Form. Gebe den Kuppelartig gewölbten Deckel darauf und bestreue es mit Parmesan und gebe es so heiss als möglich zu Tisch.

Paté in a Bowl

Make a puff pastry that has been folded 3–4 times. Put a rolled out piece of the dough into a mold in which you will bring the paté to the table. Bake the dough only half way [through] in a hot oven. Now make a big dome from paper on the paté. Make a border from the dough all around the edge [of the lined mold] and a dough cover and lay it on the greased paper dome. Brush it with egg and bake it in a hot oven.

In the meantime make yourself prepared [sic] the paté filling: Either young vegetables, or brains with eggs, or mushrooms with eggs. Or a real farce made from roasted veal or chicken, finely chopped, 1 veal brain roasted, 15 decagrams tongue or cooked smoked meat, all finely chopped, 3 anchovies, 3 softened rolls, 3 whole eggs, mushrooms, cockscombs. Combine it with a thick béchamel, lemon juice, ½ [wine] glass white wine, paté spice. Taste it and put it into the mold. Carefully lift the [pastry] cover, remove and discard the paper and put the farce as hot as possible into the [lined] mold. Top with the cupola-shaped arched [pastry] cover and sprinkle it with Parmesan and bring it as hot as possible to table.

———— ⊨♦⊟ ————

Kartoffel Heringspeise

Koche circa 20 Kartoffel in der Schale schäle sie rasch ab & drücke sie durch den Presser gebe dazu circa 5–6 Deca Butter, 3–4 Dotter & von den Eiweiss den Schnee. Vorher putze 3–4 St. Heringe nehme das Rückgrad heraus & alle Greten, zerschneide sie, die Heringe müssen im geputztem Zustand 1 Nacht oder einige Stunden weichen, auf ein Sieb und abtrocknen. Jetzt zertreibe die Heringsmilch gebe dazu den zerschnittenen Hering, 1 Becher dicken saueren Schmetten & aus 2 Löffel Mehl eine dicke Bechamell, mische dies mit der Heringsmilch zusammen. Jetzt gebe es in die Form wo du es auf den Tisch gibst die Kartoffel die wie ein Flaum sein müssen mache in die Mitte eine Vertiefung & giesse diese Milch herein & gebe es in eine sehr heisse Röhre, zu backen dass sich über das Ganze eine Kruste bildet & gebe es so heiss als möglich zu Tisch gebe dazu frische Semeln.

Potato Herring Dish

Boil about 20 potatoes, peel them quickly and put them through a potato ricer. Add about 5–6 decagrams butter, 3–4 egg yolks and from the [stiffly beaten] egg whites snow. Before, clean 3–4 pieces herring. Remove the backbone and all bones. Cut them. The cleaned herrings should be soaked overnight or for a few hours. Put them on a sieve and dry them. Now mash the herring milt. Add the cut up herring, 1 cup thick sour cream and from 2 spoons flour [make] a béchamel. Now put the very fluffy potatoes into a form [serving dish] in which you will bring it to the table. Make an indentation in the center, pour in this milt [herring] mixture and put it in a very hot oven until the top forms a crust. Bring to table as hot as possible. Serve with fresh rolls.

Hagebutten Mehlspeise

12 D Butter treibe mit 4 Dottern und 20 D Zucker, Zitronenschale, 15 Deca Haselnüsse, gebe dazu ein halbes Glas Hagebutten Marmelade; dann 20 D Bröseln und Schnee der Eiweiss backe es langsam.

Rose Hip Dessert

Blend vigorously 12 decagrams butter with 4 egg yolks and 20 decagrams sugar, lemon rind, 15 decagrams hazelnuts, and add half a glass rose-hip jam. Add 20 decagrams breadcrumbs and snow of [stiffly beaten] egg whites. Bake it slowly.

Kletzenbrot

Nehme ¼ kg gedörrte Birnen, koche selbe nur einwenig in starkem Zuckerwasser auf. Entferne das Kernhaus und zerschneide die Birnen nudelig. Ebenfalls ¼ kg gedörrte Pflaumen nicht zu weich kochen, entkernen und zerschneiden; das Wasser davon seihe durch und hebe es auf. Jetzt nehme ¼ kg Feigen, ¼ kg entkernte Blockdatteln, ¼ kg Rosinen, Zitronad, Orangenschale, Zitronenschale, alle Arten Zuckerobst in allen Farben. Gebe dazu 1 gr. Löffel Zimt, etwas Nelken, Neugewürz, Ingwer, ¼ kg Kristallzucker, ¼ kg heissen Honig, ¼ kg Fett, entweder Sana oder Butter, was beliebt, 1 Glas Rum, ¼ kg Mandeln, ¼ kg Nüsse und lasse dies über Nacht stehn [sic].

Jetzt mache einen ganz gewöhnlichen Hefeteig auf dieses Obstquantum, aus ung. [efähr] 80 D-1 kg Mehl lasse den Teig aufgehen und man kann statt Milch den schwarzen Obstsaft verwenden. Arbeite den Obststeig, Obstsaft klein Löffelweise in den Teig ein; gebe es als einen Wecken geformt auf ein beschmiertes Blech und lasse es 3 Stunden gehen & backe es langsam lasse es gebacken 2 Tage am Blech erkalten, da es leicht bricht. Obenauf kann man es mit Butter und Ei bestreichen und mit ganzen gebrühten Mandeln belegen. Zerschneide es den 3–4 Tag & gebe es in eine Blechdose. Man kann daraus auch kleine Wecken portioniert für eine Person machen.

Kletzen Bread [Fruit Bread]

Take ¼ kilogram dried pears and boil them a little in strong sugar water [syrup]. Remove core and cut pears like noodles [into strips]. Also boil ¼ kilogram prunes; not too soft. Pit them and cut them. Strain the water [syrup] and reserve. Now take ¼ kilogram [dried] figs, ¼ kilogram pitted block dates [probably dates packed together tightly], ¼ kilogram raisins, candied citron, orange and lemon peel and all kinds of sugar [candied] fruits in various colors. Add 1 large spoon cinnamon, some ground cloves, allspice, ginger, ¼ kilogram coarse sugar, ¼ kilogram hot honey, ¼ kilogram fat, either Sana [margarine] or butter, whatever is preferred, 1 glass rum, ¼ kilogram almonds, ¼ kilogram nuts. Let it stand overnight. Now make a simple yeast dough. For this amount of fruit mixture, use about 80 decagrams to 1 kilogram flour. Let the dough rise. Instead of milk, the reserved black fruit juice [syrup] can be used. Work the fruit dough [author probably meant fruit "mixture"] by small spoonfuls into the dough. Put it [the dough], shaped like a Wecken [long loaf], onto a greased baking sheet. Let it rise for 3 hours & bake it slowly. Let it cool on the baking sheet for 2 days. It breaks easily. One can brush it on top with butter and egg and stud it with blanched whole almonds. On the third or fourth day, slice it and put it into a tin box. Out of it one can apportion small Wecken [loaves] for one person.

Baierisch Brod

4 ganze Eier werden mit der Schneerute mit 35 D Zucker, Zitronen-
saft & Schale, alles schwarze Gewürz, Zimt, Nelken, Neugewürz,
tüchtig geschlagen ¼ Stunde lang dann kommt dazu 2 Tafel Choko-
lade [sic] grob gehackt, 20 Deca grob geschnittene Mandelnod. Nüsse,
& 20 Deca Zitronad [sic] & zuletzt 40 Deca Mehl. Aufs Blech
werden Oblatten belegt & diese Masse aufgegossen, gebacken & noch
warm in längliche Stücke 2 cm breit & 6 cm lang geschnitten.

Bavarian Bread

4 whole eggs with 35 decagrams sugar, lemon juice & rind, all
black spices—cinnamon, cloves, allspice—are beaten thoroughly with a whisk for ¼ hour. Then 2 tablets chocolate,
coarsely chopped, 20 decagrams coarsely cut almonds or nuts,
20 decagrams candied lemon peel and 40 decagrams flour are
added. The oblaten [white edible wafer papers] are put onto a
baking sheet & this thick mass is poured on, baked & while still
warm, cut into oblong pieces 2 centimeters wide & 6 centimeters long.

Zwetschken Strudel

*Mache eine Strudelteig mit 1 Ei etwas Fett und Mehl und lasse ihn
unter einem erwarmten Topf rasten. Jetzt weiche 3 Semmeln in Milch
bis selbe ganz aufgeweicht sind, gebe sie in eine Schüssel. Gebe dazu
15 Deca Butter, 30 Deca Zucker, einen Löffel Zimt, Zitronenschale,
4 Dotter, 15 Deca gerieben Haselnüsse & von den 4 Eiweiss Schnee,
mische diese Masse gut zusammen. Ziehe jetzt den Strudelteig etwas
stärker aus als den gewöhnlichen, streiche die Masse auf den selben
& bestreue es mit Zwetschken die auf Nudeln zerschnitten und ungef.
auf dieses Quantum 1½ kg., rolle den Strudel zusammen backe ihn
in heisser Röhre muss hoch & schön werden.*

Plum Strudel

Make a strudel dough with 1 egg, some fat and flour, and let it
rest under a heated pot. Now soak 3 rolls in milk until they are
very soft. Put them in a bowl. Add 15 decagrams butter, 30 decagrams sugar, 1 spoon cinnamon, lemon rind, 4 egg yolks, 15 decagrams ground hazelnuts, and from the 4 [stiffly beaten] egg whites
snow. Mix this mass [batter] together well. Now stretch the
dough a little thicker than usual. Spread on it the [nut] mass
[mixture] and sprinkle it with prune plums cut into noodles
[noodle shape]. For this quantity, about 1½ kilograms plums
[prune]. Roll strudel and bake in a hot oven; should be high &
beautiful.

Pomerische Gansbrust

Von einer schweren Gans, nehme den Beilik. Schneide von beiden Seiten das Fleisch, reibe es mit zertriebenem Knoblauch, etwas Salz, ½ halber Würfel Zucker zerreiben, bisschen Ingwer, gut einklopfen mit der blossen Hand und lasse es stehen. Jetzt nehme die schöne Ganshaut, lege das Beilik fleisch hinein und nähe die Ganshaut rings herum fest ein gebe sie in einen glassierten irdenen Topf und bestreue es mit bischen Salz, Potasche & Salpeter; beschwere es mit einem Teller & Gewicht und lasse es in der Beize 4 Wochen liegen & wende es täglich. Gebe es auf 2 Tage in den Selchofen dem Selcher. Man kann es auch zum Selcher in die Beize geben und lasse es schön braun selchen.

Breast of Goose, Pommern Style

From a heavy goose, take [remove] the beilik [breast]. Cut the meat from both sides, rub it with mashed garlic, some salt, ½ half sugar cube, a little ginger. Pound it [the mixture] in well with [your] bare hand and let it stand. Now take the nice skin, place the [seasoned] beilik on the skin and tightly sew the goose skin around. Put it into a glazed earthenware pot, sprinkle it with a little salt, potassium and saltpeter. Cover the breast with a plate & weights and let it lay in the brine for 4 weeks, turning it daily. Give it to the selcher [pork butcher/sausage maker] for 2 days [to put in] the smoker. One can also bring the goose breast to the pork meat butcher and let him cure and smoke it until it is nicely brown.

Chokoladen [sic] Strudel oder Kapuziener Strudel

Mache einen Strudelteig ziehe denselben etwas stärker als sonst aus. Vorher mache folgende Masse: 15 Deca Butter mit 15 Decka Zucker, 15 Deca ger. [iebene] Haselnüsse, 15 Deca ger. Chokolade, 8 Dotter, und von den 8 Eiweiss den Schnee. Streiche diese Masse auf den Strudelteig und backe es in mässig heisser Röhre und zerschneide es lau.

Chocolate Strudel or Kapuziener Strudel

Make a strudel dough and stretch it a little thicker than usual. Beforehand make the following mixture: 15 decagrams butter with 15 decagrams sugar, 15 decagrams ground hazelnuts, 15 decagrams grated chocolate, 8 egg yolks and from the 8 [stiffly beaten] egg whites snow. Spread the mixture on the strudel dough. Bake it in a moderately hot oven, and slice it lukewarm.

━━◆━━

Nuss Zopf

Mache einen gewöhnlichen guten Hefeteig circa 60–70 Deca Mehl, 4 Deca Hefe ohne Butter. Jetzt nehme ungefähr 40 Deca Butter & 5 Deca Mehl und blättere 4 mal den Teig & lasse ihn rasten. Jetzt mache eine feine Nussfülle mit viel Rosinen, etwas heisser Butter, Zucker, 1 Löffel ger. Chokolade [sic] und was man noch will. Nehme den aufgegangen Teig. Teile ihn in 3 gleiche Teile. Walke einen Teil aus gebe genau 1/3 der Nussfülle darauf und rolle es Strudelartig zusammen, und verfahre es mit allen 3 Teilen. Jetzt nehme einen Teil walke ihn in der entgegensetzen Richtung aus wie erst, verfahre so mit allen 3 Teilen jetzt walke die Teile strickartig aus; flechte daraus einen 3 teiligen Zopf; lasse es 2 Stunden gehen bestreiche es mit Butter und Ei und backe es in heisser Röhre und mache darauf eine Zuckerglasur.

Nut Braid

Make an ordinary good yeast dough from 60–70 decagrams flour, 4 decagrams yeast, without butter. Now take approximately 40 decagrams butter and 5 decagrams flour and leaf it [fold the dough like puff pastry 4 times and let it rest]. Now make a fine nut filling with a lot of raisins, a little hot butter, sugar, 1 spoon grated chocolate and anything desired. Take the risen dough and divide it into 3 equal parts. Roll out one part, spread it with exactly one third of the nut filling, and roll it together like a strudel. Repeat with remaining 2 parts and nut filling. Now take one part and roll it in the opposite direction. Repeat same with remaining 2 parts. Now roll parts into long thin strips and braid the strips together. Let the nut braid rise for 2 hours. Brush it with butter and egg and bake it in a hot oven. Make [spread] a sugar icing on top.

Wasserbett Teig

½ kg Mehl, 12 dkg Butter, 5 dkg Hefe. Aus dem Germ macht man ein Dampfl. Die Butter reibt man mit Reibeisen, Rum, Zitronen-schale, Salz und aus all dem macht man einen festen Teig ohne jede Flüssigkeit recht fest. Den Teig in einer Serviette gewickelt, die Enden zusammen binden. Gib es in einen Weidling bisschen kaltes Wasser auf eine Stunde gelegt. Man kann alles damit machen.

Waterbed Dough

½ kilogram flour, 12 decagrams butter, 5 decagrams yeast. Make a sponge from yeast. The butter is grated on a grater. [Add] rum, lemon rind, salt. Out of all one makes a stiff dough without any liquid. Roll the dough into a napkin. Tie the ends together. Lay it [the dough] in a Weidling [a large bowl] [with] a little cold water for 1 hour. One can do everything with it [the dough].

Kapuziner Nockerl (Suppe)

*3 Eiweiß Schnee, 1 Dotter, Salz, Pfeffer, Semmelbrösel in lockeren
Teig machen. Kleine Nockerln in Fett heiß backen in Rindsuppe
servieren.*

Kapuziner Dumplings (for Soup)

Snow from 3 [stiffly beaten] egg whites, 1 egg yolk, salt, pepper
and breadcrumbs to make a loose dough. [Form] small dumplings. Fry them in hot fat. Serve in beef soup [a broth].

[Recipe for use of Agar]

Agar zu Gelee in allem zu verwenden. Agar wird über Nacht in Zuckerwasser weichen gelassen, nächsten Tag weich gekocht bis es weich gekocht ist. Zu Torten Kleingebäck u. zu Fisch zu verwenden. Apfelmehlspeise [n] werden vorher mit Zucker bestreut u. mit Agar begossen.

Agar for jelly to be used for [coating] everything. Agar is left overnight in sugar water to soften. Next day it is soft cooked until it is soft cooked. To be used for cakes, small pastries, and fish. Apple desserts [cakes] are sprinkled with sugar before pouring on [dissolved and cooked] agar.

—▪ ▤◆▤ ▪—

Heu und Stroh

Mache einen Nudelteig aus ½ Kg. Mehl, 2 Eier, 2–3 Esslöffel Weisswein, 2–3 Löffel dicken sauren Schmetten. Walze die Nudeln mittelstark aus. Schneide kurze Nudeln, backe selbe in heissem Fett aus. Nehme sie heraus gebe sie in eine Auflaufschüssel bestreu sie mit Zucker, Zimt u. viel Rosinen. Jetzt mach eine feine Vanille Creme gebe dazu etwas rohen Schmetten, giesse dies über die gebackenen Nudeln gebe es in eine heisse Röhre und überbacke es und gebe es in der Form zu Tisch.

Hay and Straw

Make a noodle dough from ½ kilogram flour, 2 eggs, 2–3 tablespoons white wine, 2–3 tablespoons thick sour cream. Roll out the dough medium thick. Cut short noodles and fry them in hot fat. Remove them and put them into a soufflé dish. Sprinkle them with sugar, cinnamon and many raisins. Now make a delicate vanilla cream, add a little raw [uncooked] cream and pour over fried noodles. Put the dish into a hot oven and bake it a little. Bring to table in dish.

Gries [sic] Auflauf (Fr. Weil)

Eisen recht dicken Grießbrei kochen. Dann treibt man 10 dkg Butter, 20 dkg Zucker, 4 Dotter gut ab, in den ausgekühlten Brei gut verrühren, 10–15 dkg Arrancini und den Schnee, bißchen Backpulver, Vanillezucker u. Rum u. zu dem Schnee bißchen rohen Grieß. Langsam backen und fest bestreuen.

Farina Soufflé (Mrs. Weil)

Cook a very thick farina mush. Then vigorously cream 10 decagrams butter, 20 decagrams sugar and 4 egg yolks well. Stir into cooled mush. Mix well. [Fold in] 10–15 decagrams arrancini [chopped candied orange peel], and [egg whites stiffly beaten to] snow, a little baking powder and vanilla sugar and rum. Into snow [fold] a little raw [uncooked] farina. Bake slowly and sprinkle generously [probably with confectioners' sugar].

Mazeloksch.

Mache einen Plevedeig aus 8 Dotter
20 Deca Zucker Zitronenschale
den Schnee von den Eiweiss (ohne Mehl)
Jetzt schmiere eine Casseroll mit
Gansfett, befeuchte dünne Mazen
mit Wein oder Wasser, lege
eine Lage Mazes in die Form
betropfe es tüchtig mit heissen
Gansfetten bestreue es mit
grobgehackten Mandln, Zimt
+ gresse darauf von den Plevedeig
+ wieder verfahre mit den Mazen
so oft als es geht + immer mit
heissen Gansfett betroffen. So viel
als man den Plevedeig hat es
sollen ungef 8–9 Lagen oder
+ backe es in heisser Röhre.

Mazeloksch

Mache einen Pleweteig aus 8 Dotter, 20 Deca Zucker, Zitronen-schale, den Schnee von den Eiweiss (ohne Mehl). Jetzt schmiere ein Casseroll mit Gansfett, befeuchte dünne Mazen mit Wein oder Wasser, lege eine Lage Mazes in die Form, betropfe es tüchtig mit heissem Gansfett, bestreue es mit grobgehackten Mandeln, Zimt, u. giesse darauf von dem Pleweteig & wieder verfahre mit den Mazen so oft als es geht immer mit heissem Gansfett betropfen. So viel als man den Pleweteig hat. Es sollen ungef. 8–9 Lagen sein und backe es in heisser Röhre.

Mazeloksch

Make a Plewe cake batter [similar to sponge-cake batter] from 8 egg yolks, 20 decagrams sugar, lemon rind, snow from the [stiffly beaten] egg whites. (Without flour.) Now grease a mold [baking dish] with goose fat, dampen thin matzos with wine or water. Into the mold [baking dish], put a layer of matzos. Sprinkle it generously with hot goose fat, coarsely chopped almonds, cinnamon. Pour on some of the batter, and continue with matzos, almonds and cinnamon, as many [layers] as one has batter. Always sprinkle with hot goose fat. As many [layers] as one has batter [sic: repetition]. There should be 8–9 layers. Bake in a hot oven.

Nusstangerl

12 dkg Zucker, 14 dkg ger. Nüsse, 1 Ei, Vanille, Teig am Brett kneten, auswalzen in kleine 4 Ecke schneiden, welche mit Zitronenglasur bestreichen. In gut heisses Rohr geben.
Zitronenglasur: ¼ kg Zucker, bißchen Zitronensaft, bißchen heisses Wasser (sehr dick) gut abrühren.

Nut Sticks

12 decagrams sugar, 14 decagrams ground nuts, 1 egg, vanilla. Knead dough on board. Roll out, cut into 4 small corners [squares], spread some with lemon icing. Put into a good hot oven.
Lemon icing: ¼ kilogram sugar, a little lemon juice, a little hot water, stir well. [Icing should be very thick].

Wiener Knödel (Fr. Weil)

6 in Würfel geschnittene Semmeln, ¼ l heisse Milch, 1 Löffel But-
ter über die Semmel giessen und durchmischen. Überkühlt 2 Eier
bißchen Salz. Dazu Mehl soviel es faßt, stehen lassen. Knödel formen,
vor dem Essen 8–10 Min. kochen lassen mit Zimt u. Zucker bestreuen
oder zum Braten servieren.

Viennese Dumplings (Mrs. Weil)

Pour over 6 rolls cut into cubes, ¼ liter hot milk, 1 spoon butter. Mix well. When cooled, add 2 eggs, a little salt, and as much
flour as it absorbs. Let stand. Form dumplings and before the
meal, boil 8–10 minutes. Sprinkle dumplings with cinnamon
and sugar, or serve [plain] with roasts.

Erdäpfel Dalken

30 dkg ger. kalte Kartoffeln, 30 dkg Mehl, 3 dkg Hefe, bißchen Salz. Hefe zu einem Dampferl machen und daraus einen festen Teig gut ausarbeiten. Sofort ½ cm dicke Dalken ausstechen, 2 Stunden gehen lassen und in Fett (Öl) ausbacken. Obenauf Marmelade bestreichen und mit Zucker bestreuen.

Potato Dalken
[Doughnuts without Holes]

30 decagrams grated cold potatoes, 30 decagrams flour, 3 decagrams yeast, a little salt. Make a sponge with yeast, and with it, make a stiff dough and work it well. Immediately, cut out Dalken [rounds] ½ centimeter [$1/3$–inch] thick. Let them rise for 2 hours and fry them in fat (oil). On top spread jam and sprinkle with sugar.

Topfen Mehlspeise (warm)

25 dkg Topfen, 25 dkg Mehl, 10 dkg Zucker, 1 Ei, 2 dkg Hefe, (Dampferl) festen Teig machen, gehen lassen. Auswalken schiefe Streifen radeln, nochmals gehen lassen u.in Fett ausbacken. Vanillezucker bestreuen.

Curd Dessert (Warm)

From 25 decagrams curd, 25 decagrams flour, 10 decagrams sugar, 1 egg, 2 decagrams yeast (sponge) make a stiff dough, let rise. Roll out. With [pastry] wheel make diagonal strips. Let rise again and fry in fat. Sprinkle with vanilla sugar.

Vanille Torte

5 Dotter, 20 dkg Zucker, gut abtreiben, ½ Stange Vanille, herein reiben, 20 dkg gerieben Hasselnüsse von 5 Eiweiß Schnee. Erkaltet 1–2 Mal durchgeschnitten mit Marillenjam gefüllt, obenauf Schlagsahne.

Vanilla Cake

Stir well 5 egg yolks, 20 decagrams sugar. Grate in ½ vanilla bean. Add 20 decagrams ground hazelnuts and 5 egg whites [stiffly beaten to] snow. When cool, cut cake through once or twice. Fill with apricot jam and on top whipped cream.

Eiweiß Schnitten

6 Eiweiß Schnee, 16 dkg ger. Mandeln, 14 dkg Zucker, 5 dkg gl.
Mehl, sehr gut mischen und auf das gef. Blech. Warm in 3 Streifen
schneiden und mit folgender Fülle füllen: ⅛ 1 Milch, 8 dkg gl. Mehl,
kocht man einen Brei. 14 dkg Butter, 14 dkg Zucker, Vanille, Rum
gut abtreiben und den überkühlten Brei gut treiben.

Egg White Slices

Mix thoroughly 6 [egg whites stiffly beaten to] snow, 16
decagrams ground almonds, 14 decagrams sugar, 5 decagrams
[smooth] flour [similar in texture to all-purpose flour], mix thoroughly and [spread] on a greased baking sheet. While still warm
cut into 3 strips and fill with following filling: ⅛ liter milk with
8 decagrams flour is cooked to a mush. 14 decagrams butter, 14
decagrams sugar, vanilla, rum [is] stirred well and [added to] the
cooled mush. Stir well.

Eis à la Melba

Mache aus 1 Liter Milch, 4 Dotter, 20 Deca Zucker, Vanille eine gefrorene Masse. Gebe es in Gläser. Gebe darauf Schlagsahne, und einen halben Pfirsich aus dem Weck. Jetzt mache eine dicke feine Chokolad [sic] Crème und giesse es heiss über das Eis, aber so, dass sowohl das Eis als auch die Schlagsahne und der obenaufgelegte Pfirsich gut zu sehen ist.

Ice [Cream] à la Melba

Make a frozen mixture from 1 liter milk, 4 egg yolks, 20 decagrams sugar and vanilla. Pour it into glasses. Top it with whipped cream and a home-canned peach half. Now make a thick fine chocolate cream and pour it hot over the ice [cream], so that both the whipped cream and the peach half on the top are visible.

Forelle Reis

Koche in 1 Liter Milch den besten
Reis vorsichtig dass er sich
nicht zerkocht, er muss
weich u. sehr fest sein
Jetzt gebe es in die Schüssel
gebe dazu vorher aufgelöste
Gelatine, 50 Deca Zucker
Citronensaft 1 Glas Maraschino
1/2 Liter geschlagene Schlagsahne Vanille, jetzt
gebe dazu entkernte
eingelegte Kirschen
Erdbeeren wenn möglich
Stückchen Ananas, gebe
es in eine Gefrierform
lasse es über Nacht aus
Stürze es den nächsten
Tag aus u. gebe es mit Hohlhippen
verziert zur Tafel

Früchte Reis

Koche in 1 Liter Milch den besten Reis vorsichtig, dass er sich nicht zerkocht; er muss weich und sehr fest sein. Jetzt gebe es in die Schüssel gebe dazu vorher aufgelöste Chelatine [sic], 50 Deca Zucker, Zitronenschale, 1 Glas Maraschino, ½ Liter geschlagene Schlagsahne, Vanille. Jetzt gebe dazu eingelegte Kirschen, Erdbeeren, wenn möglich Stückchen Ananas; gebe es in eine Gefrierform. Lasse es über Nacht am Eis stehen. Stürze es den nächsten Tag aus und gebe es mit Hohlhippen zur Tafel.

Rice with Fruits

Cook the best rice carefully in 1 liter milk so that it doesn't over-cook—until the rice is tender, but [still] very firm. Now put it into a bowl. Add previously dissolved gelatin, 50 decagrams sugar, lemon rind, 1 glass maraschino [liqueur], ½ liter whipped heavy cream, vanilla. Now add home-canned cherries, straw-berries, if possible pineapple pieces. Put it into an ice cream mold. Keep it on ice overnight. Unmold it the next day and bring to the table with thin rolled wafers.

Pächters Pyrogen

Mache einen Nudelteig und walke ihn aus. Gebe jetzt gekochte geriebene Kartoffeln, zerhackte Grammeln und gebräunte Zwiebel. Fülle damit die Tascherln, drücke sie auf den Enden zu & koche sie und begiesse sie mit Fett und viel gebräunten Zwiebeln.

Pächter's Pirogen

Make a noodle dough and roll it out. Now take boiled grated potatoes, chopped cracklings and browned onions. Fill the pockets [squares], press the edges together and boil them [the pockets]. Pour hot fat and a lot of browned onion [over the pirogen].

Eis Parfée

*Mache ein Gefrorenes folgender Weise. Löse 6 Tafeln Chelatine [sic]
auf gebe es in 1½ Liter Milch 50 Deca Zucker Vanillie & 6 Dotter
dies koche auf & stelle es weg, jetzt gebe in einen Teil aufgekochte
Chokolade, in einen Teil 1 Glas starken Kaffee & in einen Teil
entweder frische Himbeere[n] oder Erdbeere[n] & den einen Teil lasse
ungefärbt. Gebe alles in eine Form, dass jeder Teil für sich halb friert.*

Ice [Cream] Parfait

Make ice cream the following way. Dissolve 6 tablets gelatin,
put it in 1½ liters milk, 50 decagrams sugar, vanilla & 6 egg yolks.
Bring it to a boil and set it aside. Now put in one part melted
chocolate, in one part 1 glass strong coffee & in one part fresh
raspberries or strawberries, & one part leave uncolored. Put everything in a mold so that each part freezes partially.

Billiger Kaffee Crêm

Koche ½ Glas Wasser mit 5–6 Blatt Gelatine auf und gebe es in den Schneekessel. Gebe dazu 2 Dotter, 10 Deca Zucker ein Glas guten schwarzen Caffee ½ L. Schlage es mit der Schneeruthe bis es ganz dick ist und gebe es in Gläser. Gebe darauf das zu Schnee geschlagene Eiweiss dem man 10 Deca Zucker etwas Vanille Geschmack beifügt und stelle es in den Eisschrank bis es fest ist. Gebe es zur Tafel mit Waffeln oder Hohlhippen verziert.

Cheap Coffee Cream

Cook ½ glass water with 5–6 gelatin leaves and pour it into a snow kettle [copper egg white bowl]. Add 2 egg yolks, 10 decagrams sugar and 1 glass good [strong] black coffee ½ liter. Beat it with a whisk until it is very thick and put it into glasses. Top with snow [2 egg whites beaten stiffly] to which 10 decagrams sugar and a little vanilla flavor is added. Put [glasses] into an ice box until it is stiff. Bring to table decorated with wafers or thin curled wafers.

Gulasch mit Nudeln

Mache aus 2 Eiern Suppennudeln und koche selbe, seihe sie ab. Gebe sie in die Schüssel gebe dazu den unterdessen gemachte Paprika ohne Sauce, viel Petersilie und gebe dazu 2 Dotter und von 2 Eiweiss Schnee gebe alles in die ausgeschmierte & ausgestreute Puding Kochform. Koche es ½ Stunde im Dunst, gebe obenauf Petersilie und etwas Parmesan und stürze es aus. Gebe es heiß zu Tisch und die verdickte Sauce vom Paprika serviere dazu.

Goulash with Noodles

Make soup noodles from 2 eggs. Boil and drain them. Put them in a bowl and add the previously prepared paprika without the sauce. [Add] a lot of parsley, 2 egg yolks and 2 [egg whites stiffly beaten to] snow. Put all into a greased and sprinkled [with breadcrumbs] pudding mold. Cook it for 30 minutes in steam. Sprinkle with parsley and a little Parmesan and unmold it. Give [bring] it hot to the table with the thickened paprika sauce.

Hühner Galantine

Nehme eine alte grosse Henne selbe darf nicht gebrüht sein unter-
meniere die Haut; vorsichtig ziehe die Haut ab und lasse sie liegen. Jetzt
löse das Fleisch von den Knochen ab, gebe dazu auch die Leber und
Magen und Herz; gebe dazu 1 Glas Weisswein etwas Paprika oder
Pfeffer, Salz, 3 ganze Eier, 3 geweichte Semmeln. Treibe das Fleisch
durch die Fleischmaschine, gebe dazu grob geschnittene, geräucherte
gekochte Zunge oder Selchfleisch, Petersilie. Arbeite alles gut durch,
schmecke es ab, jetzt nehme die Hühnerhaut, nähe die Löcher all ab.
Fülle die Haut mit der Füllung, nähe die Haut ganz zu und koche es
vorsichtig 1 Stunde lang. Gebe es dann heraus auf die Servierschüssel,
gebe in die durch gesiebte Suppe 5–6 Stücke Gelatine, etwas
Zitronensaft und seihe es ab. Den nächsten Tag, gebe diesen Aspik um
die Galantiene, garniere es mit halben harten Eiern und verziere es mit
etwas Kaviar und gebe es kalt zur Tafel. Ist sehr ausgiebig und schön.

Chicken Galantine

Take a large old hen, but do not scald her. Loosen the skin and
carefully remove the skin and let it lay. Loosen the meat from the
bones, add the liver and stomach and heart, 1 glass white wine,
some paprika or pepper, salt, 3 whole eggs, 3 softened rolls. Put
the meat through a meat grinder. Add coarsely cut smoked cooked
tongue or cooked smoked meat, parsley. Work the mixture well
and season up. Take the chicken skin and sew up all the holes.
Stuff it with the filling. Sew the skin together and boil it carefully for one hour. Remove [galantine] to a serving platter. Add
5–6 sheets gelatin to the strained broth, [and] some lemon juice
and strain it [the broth]. The next day, put this aspic around the
galantine and decorate it with hard boiled egg halves and a little
caviar. Bring it cold to the table. It is plentiful and pretty.

Gefüllte Eier [kalt] Pächter

Koche 10 Eier hart, schneide selbe durch. Nehme die Dotter heraus, passiere selbe gib dann 5 dkg Butter, 2 passierte Sardellen, etwas Senf, 3–4 Tropfen Maggi, ⅛ l geschlagenes Schlagobers, Petersilie, Zitronensaft. Nun gebe die Eier auf die Schüssel, übergiesse selbe mit Aspik vorher lasse der Fantasie freien Lauf, indem die Eier mit Schinken, Lachs, Kaviar, Kaperln verziert werden. Dann kann man die Eier in Papier Manschetten geben und serviert dazu heiße Semmelschnitten.

Cold Stuffed Eggs Pächter

Hard boil 10 eggs, cut them in half. Remove yolks and press them through a sieve. Add 5 decagrams butter, 2 anchovies pressed through a sieve, a little mustard, 3–4 drops Maggi [liquid seasoning], ⅛ liter whipped heavy cream, parsley, lemon juice. Now put eggs on a platter. Pour [liquid] aspic over. Before [pouring on the aspic] let fantasy run free and the eggs are garnished with ham, [smoked] salmon, caviar, capers. One can put the eggs into paper cuffs and serve them with hot sliced rolls.

Pächter Torte

15 dkg Zucker, 15 dkg Butter, 15 dkg ger. Haselnüsse, 10 dkg erweichte Schokolade, oder 2 Eßl. Cakau, Zitronenschale, 3 Eßl. starken schwarzen Kaffee, 2 ganze Eier, 2 Dotter, werden ¼ Stunde lang fest gerührt, dann den Schnee von den 2 Eiweiß, 20 dkg Mehl.

Pächter Cake

15 decagrams sugar, 15 decagrams butter, 15 decagrams ground hazelnuts, 10 decagrams softened chocolate or 2 tablespoons cocoa, lemon rind, 3 tablespoons strong black coffee, 2 whole eggs, 2 egg yolks are stirred vigorously for 15 minutes. Then [add] snow from the 2 [stiffly beaten] egg whites, 20 decagrams flour.

Kriegs Mehlspeise

7 gekochte geriebene Kartoffeln, 5–6 Löffel Zucker, 2 Löffel Mehl, 1 Löffel Kakau, 2 Löffel Trockenmilch, 1 Löffel [illegible], 1 Messerspitze [illegible], langsam backen.

War Dessert

7 boiled grated potatoes, 5–6 spoons sugar, 2 spoons flour, 1 spoon cocoa, 2 spoons dry milk, 1 spoon [illegible], 1 knife point [pinch] [illegible]. Bake slowly.

Omlette mit Äpfeln

*³/₈ l Milch, 25 dkg Mehl, 2 Dotter, 1 Löffel Zucker, Salz, 2 dkg Hefe,
gut versprudeln, dann 2 Klar Schnee darunter rühren. In warmen
Ort zugedeckt stehen lassen. Äpfel schälen am Reibeisen reiben,
darunter mischen. Nun mit Schöpflöffel im siedendem Fett Omletten
ausbacken, zusammen legen, gut mit Zucker u. Zimt bestreuen.*

Omelet with Apples

⅜ liter milk, 25 decagrams flour, 2 egg yolks, 1 spoon sugar, salt,
2 decagrams yeast, mix well. Then stir in 2 egg whites [stiffly
beaten to] snow. Let stand covered in a warm place. Peel and
grate apples on a grater to mix in [to batter]. Now with a ladle
[of batter poured] into boiling fat, fry omelets. Fold and sprinkle
well with sugar and cinnamon.

Kartoffel Kuchen

35 dkg Mehl, ¼ kg gek. ger. Kartoffeln, 10 dkg flüssige Margarine, 1 Ei, 5 dkg Zucker, 3 dkg Hefe, Salz, 2 Tortenblätter auswalzen, 2 verschieden Füllen u. langsam backen.

Potato Kuchen

35 decagrams flour, ¼ kilogram cooked, grated potatoes, 10 decagrams melted margarine, 1 egg, 5 decagrams sugar, 3 decagrams yeast, salt. Roll out 2 cake leaves [layers]. Spread with 2 different fillings and bake slowly.

Spargel Salat

Koche ½ kg Spargelspitzen in Salzwasser dem man 1 Würfel Zucker beifügt, gebe es auf die Schüssel wo es serviert wird. Die Spitzen müssen rings um die Schüssel heraus schauen, jetzt begiesse es mit einer dicken Majonaise, belege es mit harten Eiern und Salatblättern und stelle es bis zum servieren in den Kühlschrank.

Asparagus Salad

Boil ½ kilogram asparagus points in salted water with 1 sugar cube. Put on the platter where [they] will be served. The tips must [be placed] in a circle with the points looking out [towards the edge] of the platter. Now pour a thick mayonnaise over [them]. [Garnish] with hard boiled eggs and lettuce leaves and put in the icebox until serving.

Majonaise für Spargel Salat

In ¼ Liter Milch gebe 2 Dotter 3 Würfel Zucker eine Prise Salz etwas Essig & etwas von dem Spargelwasser 10 Deca Butter oder 5 Esslöffel Öl 2 Esslöffel Mehl lasse dies aufkochen und gebe dazu eine Idee Zwiebel.

Mayonnaise for Asparagus Salad

Into ¼ liter milk, put 2 egg yolks, 3 sugar cubes, a pinch salt, some vinegar and some asparagus water [water in which the asparagus were cooked], 10 decagrams butter or 5 tablespoons oil, 2 tablespoons flour. Bring it to a boil and add a touch of onion.

Eiswürfel (Fr. Krejsky)

¼ kg weisses Kunerol erweichen lassen. 10 dkg Zucker, 2 ganze Eier, 1 Kaffeelöffel Kakao, 4 Rippchen erweichte Schokolade, ¼ kg Studentenfutter, bißchen Salz alles zusammen mischen. Blech oder Form mit weissen Oblatten auslegen. Masse aufgiessen und erstarren lassen. Kalt stellen und nach Belieben schneiden.

Ice Cubes (Mrs. Krejsky)

Soften ¼ kilogram white Kunerol [shortening], add 10 decagrams sugar, 2 whole eggs, 1 coffeespoon cocoa, 4 ribs [crosswise divisions of a European chocolate bar] softened chocolate, ¼ kilogram Studentenfutter [student food, i.e., mixed dried fruits and nuts], a little salt. Mix all together. Line a baking sheet or cake pan with edible wafer paper. Pour on fruit mass and let harden. Put in a cold place and cut into pieces as desired.

Milchrahmstrudel

Fülle: ¼ 1 Rahm, 2 Dotter 6 dkg gesch. ger. Mandeln, Zucker nach Geschmack, 1 in Milch geweichte Semmel, 4 dkg Butter, alles abtreiben, 2 Klar Schnee, Rosinen streuen leicht backen mit gezuckerter Milch übergießen, verdünsten lassen. In einem Kasserol backen.

Milk-Cream Strudel

Filling: ¼ liter cream, 2 egg yolks, 6 decagrams blanched, ground almonds, sugar to taste, 1 roll soaked in milk, 4 decagrams butter, all beaten. 2 whites snow [stiffly beaten egg whites]. Sprinkle with raisins, bake lightly. Pour over sugared milk. Let it evaporate. Bake in a casserole [baking dish]. [Recipe for strudel dough is omitted.]

Torte (*sehr gut*)

4 große rohe geriebene Kartoffeln oder gelbe Rüben, 4 große Eßlöffel Haferflocken, 3 Eß[löffel] Kaffee Ersatz, 5 Eß[löffel] Zucker, 1 Messer-spitze Soda, 1 Pernikpulver, etwas Aroma. Mit Crem füllen und glasieren.

Torte (Very Good)

4 large raw grated potatoes or carrots, 4 large tablespoons rolled oats, 3 tablespoons coffee substitute, 5 tablespoons sugar, a pinch baking soda, 1 packet gingerbread spice powder, a little flavoring. Fill with cream and glaze.

—◄◆►—

Busserln

2 Tassen Haferflocken, 2 Tassen Mehl, 1 Tasse Zucker, 3–5 dkg Sana, 1 Tasse Milch, 1 Backpulver oder Soda, (1 Ei). Kugerln formen in die Mitte eine Vertiefung u. Marmelade.

Kisses

2 cups rolled oats, 2 cups flour, 1 cup sugar, 3–5 decagrams Sana [margarine], 1 cup milk, 1 [packet] baking powder or baking soda, (1 egg). Shape into small balls. In center [put] an indentation and fill with jam.

Gesundheits Kuchen Bäckers

24 Deca Zucker 24 Deca Butter 6 Deca
geröste ger. Mandl 1 Deca Bittere
Zitronenschale 6 Dotter werden ½ Stunde
gerührt, dann 1½ Kaffeebecher voll
süssen Schmetten 48 Deca griffiges
Mehl vermischt mit 18 Gramm
Natron & 8 Gramm Weinstein & aus
den 6 Eiweiss der Schnee, gebe
es in die ausgeschmierte & aus=
gestreute Kugelnupfform & backe
es langsam bei mässiger
Hitze 1¼ Stunde. — Es ist zuviel
die Hälfte in der form & muss die
grosse form ganz hoch & voll werden

Gesundheits Kuchen (Pächters)

24 Deca Zucker, 24 Deca Butter, 6 Deca gebrühte, ger. Mandl 1 Deca Bittere, Zitronenschale, 6 Dotter werden ½ Stunde gerührt, dann 1½ Kaffeebecher voll süssen Schmetten, 48 Deca griffiges Mehl vermischt, 18 Gramm Natron, & 8 Gramm Weinstein und aus den 6 Eiweiss den Schnee; gebe es in die ausgeschmierte und ausgestreute Kugelhupfform und backe es langsam bei mässiger Hitze 1¼ Stunden. Es ist ungef[ähr] die Hälfte in der Form und muss die grosse Form ganz hoch und voll werden.

Healthcake (Pächter's)

Stir 24 decagrams sugar, 24 decagrams butter, 6 decagrams blanched, ground almonds, 1 decagram [ground] bitter [almonds], lemon rind, 6 egg yolks, for half an hour. Then stir in 1½ coffee cups cream, 48 decagrams flour, 18 grams baking soda and 8 grams cream of tartar, and from the 6 egg whites snow [stiffly beaten whites]. Pour the batter into the buttered and floured Kugelhopf mold and bake slowly at moderate heat for 1¼ hours. The [cake] pan should be about half full of it [the batter], and should be full and rise to the top [when baked].

Badener Caramell Bonbons

30 Deca Zucker ohne Wasser bräunen, giesse dazu ⅓ Liter Caffeextract, ⅛ Liter Schmetten, und wenn dies verkocht ist 8 Deca Theebutter [sic] und lasse es kochen bis es Dick flüssig ist . Giesse es kochend in die mit Butter ausgestrichene Zuckerlnform und mit dem umgekehrtem Messer zerteile es ehe es ganz erkaltet. Dann zerbreche es in Würfel und packe es in Pergamentpapier und noch in rosa Papier damit.

Caramels from Baden

Brown [caramelize] 30 decagrams sugar without water. Pour in ⅓ liter coffee extract [very strong coffee], ⅛ liter cream and bring it to a boil. Add 8 decagrams tea butter [best quality butter] and cook until mixture is thick. Pour boiling into a buttered candy pan. With the back of a knife divide it before it completely cools. Then break it into cubes and wrap in parchment and also pink paper.

Caramell Crême

50 Deca Zucker nur mit 1 Löffel Wasser bräunen, giesse dazu 1 Liter starken schwarzen Caffee bis das verkocht ist, giesse dazu 1 Dose dicke Kondenzmilch. Lasse es unter immer währenden Rühren stark verkochen gebe dazu 10 Deca Theebutter [sic] und bis es die Dicke von einem Brei erreicht hat, gebe es heiß in die dazu bestimmten Gefässe.

Caramel Cream

Brown [caramelize] 50 decagrams sugar, with only 1 spoon water. Pour in 1 liter strong black coffee and boil [until sugar is incorporated]. Pour in 1 can thick condensed milk. Stirring constantly, boil vigorously until liquid is reduced. Add 10 decagrams tea butter [best quality butter], and cook stirring until mixture is very thick and the consistency of brei [mush]. Pour hot into designated containers.

Glasieren der Früchte

Die Früchte anwärmen, dann auf Sieb heraus geben, mit frischem Zucker zum Faden (Thermometer 87 Grad) übergiessen und einmal aufgekocht. Dann Zucker ableeren, 2 Tage wiederholen, dann die Früchte auf Sieben abtropfen lassen. Zum Glasieren 5 Kg Zucker, 10 dkg Syrup bis 90–91 Grad kochen immer ein Teil Früchte hineingeben, am Kesselrand etablieren, 1 Minute heiss abtrocknen, Früchte auf Gitter überziehen, in mittelwarmen Trockenschrank 8 Stunden stehen lassen, dann heraus nehmen, 1 Tag kalt stehen lassen und dann reihenweise in Kartons oder Kisteln packen. Wenn so gearbeitet, garantiere Erfolg.

Glazing Fruits

Warm fruits. Put them on a sieve, pour [over them] fresh sugar [syrup] boiled to a thread (87 degrees on a thermometer) [approximately 224° F] and bring to a boil once. Then empty [drain] sugar [syrup]. Repeat for 2 days. Then let fruits drain on sieves. For glazing: 5 kilograms sugar, 10 decagrams syrup. Boil to 90–91 degrees. Keep adding a part of [the] fruits. Stabilize fruits at edge of kettle for 1 minute. Drain syrup. Dry for 1 minute while hot. Put fruits on racks and put them in a drying closet of [medium warm temperature]. Dry them for 8 hours. Remove fruits. Let them stand for 1 day before packing them in rows in cartons or small crates. If worked in this way, [I] guarantee success.

Kandierte Früchte

1. *Tag:* *Die Früchte blangieren und weich kochen.*
2. " : *Nach dem Blangieren in 20 grädigen kalten Zucker legen, 20 Grad ist ½ kg Zucker in einem ein viertel Liter Wasser lösen.*
3. " : *10 dkg Zucker zugeben, aufkochen und ausgekühlt über die Früchte giessen.*
4. " : *Den Zucker abgiessen, wieder 10 dkg Zucker zugeben, aufkochen und kalt über die Früchte giessen.*
5. " : *den Zucker aufkochen, abschäumen und die Früchte mit aufkochen.*
6. " : *25 dkg Syrup dem Zucker beifügen, aufkochen und mit den Früchten an einem warmen Ort über Nacht stehen lassen.*
7. " : *Dasselbe wiederholen bis zum grossen Faden. Somit ist die Frucht zum Glasieren vorbereitet und muss bis zu 3 Monaten im Zucker liegen, damit sie recht gesättigt wird.*

Candied Fruits

1. Day: Blanch the fruits and cook till soft.
2. " : After the blanching, put them into a 20 degree cold sugar [solution]. 20 degrees are ½ kilogram sugar dissolved in 1/4 liter water.
3. " : Add 10 decagrams sugar, bring to a boil and [when] cool pour over fruits.
4. " : Strain sugar [syrup], again add 10 decagrams sugar [to it]. Bring it to a boil and pour cold over fruits.
5. " : Bring sugar to a boil, skim it and bring to a boil with fruits.
6. " : Add 25 decagrams syrup to sugar, bring it to a boil with fruits and let stand in a warm place overnight.
7. " : Repeat [the process] to the large thread stage. With this the fruit is prepared for glazing and should be kept in the sugar for 3 months to be properly saturated.

Knödel

Semmel in Würfel geschnitten, die Hälfte in Milch geweicht und stehen lassen. Die andere Hälfte in Fett geröstet. Stückerln Speck und Wurst auch abbraten. Alles zusammen geben und soviel Mehl als es nötig ist. 10–15 Minuten kochen lassen.

Dumplings

Rolls are cut into cubes. Soak half in milk and let stand. Roast the other half in fat. Also roast small pieces of bacon and sausage. Mix all together and add as much flour as needed. [Egg is missing.] Let boil for 10–15 minutes.

Korn Schnaps

½ kg Korn, es werden 2 dkg Hefe zerbröckelt, 60 dkg Zucker mit bisschen Wasser aufkochen, ausgekühlt in das Gurkenglas giessen und mit kaltem Wasser vollgiessen, dann mit Papier verschliessen u.löchern. 10 Tage am warmen Ort stehen lassen u.dann durch Leinen filtrieren u.in Flaschen füllen.

Rye Schnaps

½ kilogram rye [the grain], 2 decagrams yeast, crumbled. Bring 60 decagrams sugar with a little water to a boil. Pour cooled into a cucumber [pickle] jar and fill with water. Close [cover] it [the open jar] tightly with paper and perforate [the paper]. Let stand for 10 days in a warm place and then filter the liquid through a piece of linen and pour into bottles.

—◆─≣◆≣─◆—

Lebkuchen Caces

Im Wasserbad in einem Gefäß werden geschlagen 12 dkg Marg. 25 dkg Zucker, 25 dkg Honig, 1 Kaffeelöffel Speisesoda, alles zusammen wird solange gerührt, bis die Masse dick ist. In die ausgekühlte Masse wird eingemischt 60 dkg glattes Mehl, 1 Päckchen Lebkuchen Gewürz. Der Teig wird über Nacht rasten gelassen. Dann ganz dünn auswalgen [sic], mit dem Radl Formen machen aufs eingeschmierte Blech geben nach dem backen kalt vom Blech nehmen.

Gingerbread Cookies

In a container in a waterbath, beat together 12 decagrams margarine, 25 decagrams sugar, 25 decagrams honey, 1 coffeespoon baking soda. Beat all together until the [mixture forms] a thick mass. Into the cooled mass mix 60 decagrams flour, 1 packet gingerbread spice. Let the dough rest overnight. Then roll out very thinly. With a pastry wheel make shapes. [Place] them on a greased baking sheet. After baking, remove cold from baking sheet.

Topfenschnitten oder Torte

10½ dkg Mehl, 7 dkg Butter, 4 dkg Staubzucker, 1 Dotter werden vermengt. Auf einem Tortenblech oder Blech leicht gebacken. Dann mischt man ¼ kg Topfen, 1 Dotter, etwas Butter, Vanille und Zucker nach Geschmack, Zitronenschale, treibt dies fest ab, gibt auf die gebackene Masse. Darauf wird von 2–3 Klar fester Schnee gemacht, 4 dkg Staubzucker eingemengt und über den Topfen gegeben und 10 Minuten in der Röhre backen bis es eine leicht gelbe Farbe hat.

Curd Slices or Cake

10½ decagrams flour, 7 decagrams butter, 4 decagrams con-fectioners' sugar, 1 egg yolk are combined [and] on a cake pan or baking sheet lightly baked. Then mix ¼ kilogram curd [pot cheese], 1 egg yolk, some butter, vanilla and sugar to taste [and] lemon rind. Mix it vigorously and spread on the baked dough. Next one does make from 2–3 [beaten] egg whites stiff snow. 4 decagrams confectioners' sugar [is] mixed in and put over cheese [mixture] and bake for 10 minutes, or until it has a light yellow colour.

Makové Řezy

3 vajíčka, 14 dkg cukru , 7 dkg másla, 7 dkg mletého máku, 7 dkg ořechů, citronová štáva a kůra, sníh. Na plech namazat, upečený marmeladou plnit, povrch glasura.

Poppy Seed Slices

3 eggs, 14 decagrams sugar, 7 decagrams butter, 7 decagrams ground poppy seeds, 7 decagrams [ground] nuts, lemon juice and rind, [egg whites stiffly beaten to] snow. Spread on baking sheet. [When] baked, fill with jam, top with icing.

RECIPE LIST
FOR THE
ORIGINAL MANUSCRIPT

Note: Bracketed recipes are untitled in the original. Inconsistencies in spelling are a reflection of the manuscript.

Mürber Strudel
Flaky Strudel

[Czech Cake 1]

Ženichový Dort
Groom's Cake

Ausgiebige Schokolade Torte
Rich Chocolate Cake

Bohnen Torte
Bean Cake

Leberknödel
Liver Dumplings

Tobosch Torte
Tobosch Torte

Apfel Knödel
Apple Dumplings

Makaronen
Macaroons

Kartoffel Salat
Potato Salad

Linzer Torte
Linzer Torte

Hirse Knödel
Millet Dumplings

Butter Kindeln
Butter Kindeln

Feine Palfy Knödel
Delicate Palfy Dumplings

Ganshals mit Gries gefüllt
Goose Neck stuffed with
Farina

Kartoffel Schmarn [illegible]
Potato Schmarn [illegible]

Zwiebel Kuchen
Onion Kuchen

Winter-Salat
Winter Salad

Billige echte jüdische Bobe
Cheap Real Jewish Bobe
[Coffee Cake]

Billige Hagebutt Pusserln
Cheap Rose Hip Kisses

Schüssel Pastete
Paté in a Bowl

Kartoffel Heringspeise
Potato Herring Dish

Hagebutten Mehlspeise
Rose Hip Dessert

Kletzenbrot
Kletzen Bread

Baierisch Brod
Bavarian Bread

Zwetschken Strudel
Plum Strudel

Pomerische Gansbrust
Breast of Goose, Pommern
    Style

Chokoladén Strudel
Chocolate Strudel

Nuss Zopf
Nut Braid

Wasserbett Teig
Waterbed Dough

Kapuziner Nockerln
Kapuziner Dumplings

[Recipe for use of Agar]

Heu und Stroh
Hay and Straw

Grieß Auflauf
Farina Souffle

Kaffeecrem [illegible]
Coffee Cream [illegible]

Mazeloksch
Mazeloksch

[Recipe] [illegible]

Fleischroulade [illegible]
Meat Roulade [illegible]

Nusstangerln
Nut Sticks

Wiener Knödel
Viennese Dumplings

Erdäpfel Dalken
Potato Dalken

Topfen Mehlspeise
Curd Dessert

Vanille Torte
Vanilla Cake

Eiweiß Schnitten
Egg White Slices

Gerstenmehl Torte
Barley Flour Cake [illegible]

Eis à la Melba
Ice [Cream] a la Melba

Früchte Reis
Rice with Fruits

Pächter Torte
Pächter's Cake

Kriegs Mehlspeise
War Dessert

Gefüllte Eier (warm)
  [illegible]
Stuffed Eggs (Warm)
  [Illegible]

Pächters Pyrogen
Pächter's Pirogen

Eis Parfée
Ice [Cream] Parfait

Billigen Kaffee Creme
Cheap Coffee Cream

Gulasch mit Nudeln
Goulash with Noodles

Hühner Galantine
Chicken Galantine

Gefüllte Eier [kalt] Pächter
Cold Stuffed Eggs Pächter

Pächter [illegible]
Pächter [Illegible]

Falsche Tobosch Schnitten
  [illegible]
Mock Tobosch Slices
  [Illegible]

Majonaise for Spargel Salat
Mayonnaise for Asparagus
  Salad

Eiswürfel
Ice Cubes

Milchrahmstrudel
Milk-Cream Strudel

Omlette mit Äpfeln
Omelette with Apples

Kartoffel Kuchen
Potato Kuchen

Apfelguß [illegible]
Apple Glaze [Illegible]

Haferflocken Torte [illegible]
Oatmeal Cake [Illegible]

Spargel Salat
Asparagus Salad

Patzerl Kugelhupf
  [illegible]
Patzerl Kugelhupf
  [Illegible]

Torte (sehr gut)
Torte (Very Good)

Busserln
Kisses

Gesundheits Kuchen
Health Cake

Separate Sheets

Badener Caramell Bonbons
Caramels from Baden

Caramell Creme
Caramel Cream

Glasieren der Früchte
Glazing Fruits

Knödel
Dumplings

Lebkuchen Caces
Gingerbread Cookies

Korn Schnaps
Rye Schnaps

Topfen Schnitten oder Torte
Curd Slices or Cake

[Czech Cake 2]

Makové Řezy
Poppy Seed Strips

Grieß Knödel
Farina Dumplings

Kandierte Früchte
Candied Fruits

Kirsch-Zwetschken Knödel
Cherry-Plum Dumplings

Practical Notes

Agar—A form of dried seaweed with setting properties.

Butter—When a European recipe calls for butter, it generally means unsalted butter.

Chocolate ribs—Long crosswise strips of chocolate, as opposed to squares. More common in Europe.

Coffeespoon—A spoon smaller than a teaspoon.

Decagram—Ten grams, a metric unit equal to 0.35 ounces. In the manuscript dece, decca, d, dg, dkg are all abbreviations for decagram.

Farina—As used here, a wheat product similar in texture to semolina.

Form—Generally means a Torten Form, that is, a cake pan.

Germ—Yeast. Although most of the contributors to Mina's cookbook were probably Czech, there are a number of Austrian terms used in the recipes that may simply be the result of overlapping traditions or may indicate that the author was Austrian, says Bianca Steiner Brown. One example is the use of the Austrian-German word *Germ* for yeast, as opposed to the standard German *Hefe*.

Glattes Mehl* or *das Glätte Mehl—Smooth flour similar in texture to our all-purpose flour.

Gram—0.035 ounces.

Kilogram—1000 grams, or approximately 2.20 pounds.

Liter—Approximately 1.05 quarts.

Mehlspeise—A Middle European term for almost any kind of dessert.

Oblaten—Religious wafer sometimes used for cakes; also edible wafer paper used in baking.

Schnee—The term "snow"—that is, beaten egg whites—appears often in the recipes, usually in an extremely abbreviated form. For example, a recipe might call for 3 *Schnee* (3 egg whites beaten stiffly to snow).

Spoon—European spoons, both small and large, may vary in size. When spoon measurements are given in recipes, it is intended more as a loose indication of quantity than as precise amount.

Studentenfutter—Literally, student food; a combination of fruit and nuts similar to trail mix.

Réaumur—On the Réaumur scale, the abbreviation for which is the letter "R," 0 is the temperature at which water freezes and 80 the temperature at which it boils. The temperature of 87 degrees called for in the Glasieren der Früchte, a recipe for glazing fruits, is probably a Réaumur measurement.

Teebutter (or Theebutter)—Literally, tea butter. The very best butter.

Topfen—Curd; similar to a dry pot cheese or hoop cheese.

Weck—A preserving kettle.

POEMS

BY

WILHELMINA (MINA) PÄCHTER

Written in Terezín

Introduction and Translations
by David Stern, Grandson of Mina Pächter

INTRODUCTION

Many poems were written in Terezín, often sad or grim. Mina's came on separate sheets, not part of the cookbook. Though they try to sound humorous, they mirror reality: many women to a room, separated from their families, arguing over a few extra inches of allotted space, and perhaps "cooking platonically" (a phrase used in one of the poems that may be a reference to the writing of the cookbook). Overshadowing all this is the horror of "the East," of Auschwitz-Birkenau.

Frau Professor liegt an der Wand
Heisst wie der Cherusker
Ist aber durchaus nicht mit ihm verwandt
Sie macht Nudeln nicht nach Muster.
Geht von Hause wenns noch sehr düster.

Der Professor kommt täglich her
Früher las er den Homer
Und im Urtext: Herakles und Mark Aurel
Heute liest er nur Tagesbefehl
Und den Zettel der Menage.

Ja. In Teresín hat man Deiges* und keine Courage.
Jetzt muss ich noch von mir was sagen
Ich bin nur, kann es aber kaum wagen
Ich bin durchaus faul und gefrässig
Doch niemals gegen Jenn gehässig
Hab eine Elefantenhaut gegen Beleidigungen
Meine Indolenz hat noch Keiner bezwungen
Ich hab schon keinen Esprit und keinen Elan
Man tut zwar imer noch was man kann

Genug des Geschimpfes, Fr. Holz befiehlt
Sind wir noch eine Familie, wie man sieht
Ich lass mich nicht weiter beschimpfen, davon ein
   Glied
So muss ich schweigen und mich bescheiden
Fast fürchte ich, ich werde senil
Es geht mir imer herum im Sinn
Die baldige Abreise von Teresín

The professor's wife lies by the wall
Like the Cherusker she is called
Though not related to him at all
Makes noodles of no known mold
Leaves home in darkness before dawn.

(5)   The professor visits every day
He used to read the Odyssey
In Greek and Latin: Heracles
And works of Mark Aurelius
Now reads just daily proclamations
(10) And chits that list starvation rations.

Yes. in Terezín one has no courage, just worry.
And now I must tell you my own story
It isn't a thing that is gladly confessed
But I am lazy and with food obsessed
Yet against no one by hate possessed
(15) My elephant's skin has all insults repelled
My indolence so far no one has dispelled
I have no more spirit, have no elan
I get along as well as I can.

But no more harsh words, Mrs. Holz lays down law
(20) We still are one family, as you should know
For me, too, a member, the insults should cease
And so I withdraw, and will hold my peace
I fear meanwhile
I am almost getting senile
(25) My thoughts are forever in a spin:
I may soon depart from Terezín.

Deiges—da'agot, "worries" in Hebrew.

Januar, 1943, Theresienstadt.

V Teresíne u Prahy
Tam jsou velky kasárny*
Und Mitten zwischen von Dreien
Steht unser Haus, eines der miesen
Hier heisst es nur Ubikation
Sagen Sie mir: was ist das schon?
Als Zimmercomandantin
Regiert Frau Holz wie eine Infantin
Was heisst das, sie ruft entrüstet
Frau Langer, der Fussboden muss sein gebürstet

Doch diese empört sich, bin ich denn ein Viech
Dass ich muss reinigen allen Schmutz
Ich such mir noch eine andere Arbeit
Dann hab ich 'nen Schutz.

(eine Zeile unlesbar)

Keine Angelegenheit: anders geht es nicht
Frau Langer spricht
Bin ich denn auf einen Handgriff erpicht?
Warum sagen Sie das nicht, Fr. Weil?
Diese aber schweigend, denkt sich ihr Teil.
In ihrer nassen Ecke
Macht sie chlupaty knedliky um die Wette
Sie ist der Reinlichkeitsapostel
Wäscht, putzt und scheuert, allezeit
Trotz Kranksein ist sie in Arbeit am Posten
Gott schütze sie gnädig vor dem Osten.

Nun sind wir nicht wie eine Familie?
Ruft die Comandeuse
Wer von Euch konnte mir sein böse?
Wirklich harmonisch bis auf die Streiterei
Sehen Sie, die hat mehr als 5 Centimeters
Wegen 5 Centimeter, was ist schon dabeis
Ich muss mit der Suppe jetzt fort
Wer wird vertreten mich beim Abort?

Closetdienst wird es genannt
Das Lokal ist einer Latriene verwandt
Ein fauliges Brett, ewig bepischt
Wehe wenn die Dame vom Closetdienst Eine erwischt

Aber der Hausgewaltige . . .
Nimmt diese Sache qewichtig
Meine Damen, Dienst ist Dienst
Wenn's rein ist, ist es Ihr Verdienst
Rückehrend die Zimmerälteste spricht
Frau Wertheim, das dulde ich nicht
Sie müssen sich waschen sobald es geht
Nicht wann Sie wollen,
Sonder wenn das Wasser am Ofen steht

Erbost schnaubt diese die Befehlende an
Das geht einen Schmarn Sie an
Ich kann mich waschen wann ich will
Seien Sie still!

Ich verklag Sie beim Herrn vom Haus
Und steckt auf die Vorgesetzte,
1, 2, 3 die ganze Zunge heraus
Gut noch sie steckt nicht die avers Seite aus.

Ja, ein sanftes Lämchen war Xantipe
Verglichen dieser Adamsrippe
Beruhigt sich bald, erzählt uns von
Kaiserbesuchen & tiefen Decoltée

Damals waren vielleicht Reize vorhanden
Doch heute o weh! schon alle entschwanden
Und pfeift uns was vor wie eine Varietée.

Zwei Nachbaren hat die Dame o Graus
Vertragt sich mit ihnen wie Katze und Maus
Frau Ermes ruft. Ich will meine Ruh
Deckt sich bis über die Ohren mit der Daunendecke zu.

Den Zimerrothschild muss man respectieren
Und estimieren und hofieren
Sie hat eine gute Valuta fürwahr
Ist so sanft wie der Sturmwind
Den sie verwirklicht in Tat und Bild

Zu ihrer Schwiegernichte ist sie die sorgende Glucke
Und nimt die Schwiegermutter Pflichten sehr
    gewissenhaft
Mit Nichten es ist der Hanička nicht apropos
Aber es ist nun einmal so
Die steht noch [ein] bisl in den Flitterwochen
Will aber nicht auf diese Rechte pochen

Frau Kreisky ist ein guter Hascher
Auch die denkt sich ihr Teil und eilet rascher
Als sonst ihre Art um nicht Zeuge zu sein der Streiterei.
Was sie aber durchaus nicht bedrückt

Bei der Türe liegt ein Schwesternpaar
Harmonisch wie selten es war
Sie kochen zusammen oft nur platonisch
Zusamen geschmolzen die Vorräthe sind
Jede hat da Mann und Kind
Doch erfinderisch sind beide in diesem Fach
Imer haben sie etwas Neues erdacht
Oft schon hab ich davon versucht

Und nur das geringe Quantum verflucht
Vergebens spekuliere ich nach schwachen Seiten
Um der Liesl und Vally bisl Verlegenheit zu bereiten
Bei Gott, es fällt mir gar nichts ein
Vally, des Zimer Demosthenes ist

Doch konnt sie es trotzdem nicht erreichen
Das Herz des Haustyrannen punto Massenbelag
  zu erweichen
Jeder im Zimmer hat sie gern
Eine Schmeichelei zu sagen liegt mir fern
Liesie die Andere der Beiden
Ist auf Ehre sehr gut zu leiden
Ist meine unmittelbare Schlafgenossin
Ist eine brilliante Sopransängerin
Und eine virtuosische Flohfängerin
Hat eine Tochter eine bildschöne
Mit gewaltigen Auftritt [?]
Grauenvoll denk ich dran, wenn ich's erwähne

* Czech: In Terezín by Prague there are big barracks.

January 1943, Theresienstadt

Near Prague, in town of Terezín
Stand many barracks, big and grim
And among three in its interior
Stands our house, it's quite inferior

(5)   "Ubikation" it's called today:
What is that strange word, anyway?
As room "kommandant," ruling the scene
Mrs. Holz reigns over us like a queen
What does it mean, she shouts with a rush
(10) Mrs. Langer, the floor must be scrubbed with a
     brush!
But that one gets angry and voices her hurt:
Am I just a beast, to scrub all this dirt?

I'll seek a job in another direction
And this will give me some protection.
   [line illegible]
(15) No concern: otherwise it won't go.

Mrs. Langer speaks: just one demand
Is anyone anxious to lend me a hand?
Mrs. Weil, why do you begrudge me support?
But that one keeps out, with never a word.
(20) In her own corner, eternally wet
Makes her dumplings, as if on a bet
She is with cleanliness obsessed
Cleans, washes, scrubs without any rest
Though sick, her work has never ceased
(25) May God's grace save her from the East.

"Are we not a family?" The room kommandant
   called
"Can anyone here find in me the least fault?"
I keep harmony with everyone
Except those few too quarrelsome
(30) "Those five centimeters are not hers by right"
Five centimeters—are they worth a fight?
Now with the soup away I race
For privy duty, who takes my place?

"Toilet service" the name is officially stated
(35) The establishment to a latrine is related
A foul board, always covered with piss
Woe if the lady in charge sees you miss
But the room's potentate
Gives the matter great weight
My ladies, the work you do is not in vain

When all has been cleaned, it is your own gain
(40) The eldest of the room returns:

"Mrs. Wertheim, with this I won't abide
Wash up when you can and delay it not
Don't do it whenever you decide
(45) But when the water on the stove is hot."
The other just snorts at such demands
"I don't give a damn for your commands
I wash myself whenever I will
Shut up and be still!"

(50) "To the authorities I will complain
About you," but it is all in vain
In the room leader's face, one, two, three
Is stuck out a tongue, for all to see
Good that her other end she hasn't bared.

(55) Xanthippa a lamb was, when compared
To this Adam's rib. Yet soon she quiets down
Tells of Emperor's visit, and deep-cut-out gown.
Back then her charms may have been highly rated
But by now, alas, they have all dissipated.
(60) And a tune she can blow
Like a variety show.

Two neighbors has this lady, oh brother
Like cat and mouse they are at each other.
Mrs. Ermes calls out: be quiet, please!
(65) Under feather comforter hides to find peace.

The room's Rothschild gets flattery and respect
A currency she likes to collect

As gentle as the howling storm
That is her style, in deed and form

(70) Yet she's mother hen to her niece-in-law
And motherly favors will kindly bestow
With nieces Hanička does not seem to fit
But these are the facts, that is it.
She still enjoys her honeymoon
(75) But will not claim her rights back soon.

Mrs. Kreisky, a good soul, kind and serene
She too has her thoughts and will rush off the
    scene
As usual, out of a quarrel to stay
But none of this ever will cause her dismay.

(80) Two sisters by the door, a pair
Their harmony is something rare
A love of cooking both do share
But it's platonic, their cupboard is bare
The food they had brought no longer there.
(85) A man and child each has somewhere
Both creative in this art
Always something new they start
Often some of it I tried
Just the skimpy share decried

(90) In vain do you seek weakness or folly
That might embarrass dear Liesel or Vally
By God, not one flaw I can recall
Like Demosthenes, Vally speaks for us all
Still, all her skill and eloquent art

(95)   Will never soften our house-tyrant's heart
        Everyone gives her great appreciation
        This is no flattering exaggeration
        Liesel is the other of the two
        Easy to live with, that is true
(100) My neighbor when we lie down for the night
        A brilliant soprano whose voice is delight
        A virtuoso flea-catcher
        Her daughter pretty as a picture
        With tremendous showy tread
(105) Saying it fills my mind with dread.

Frau Heiman, wollen wir nicht übergehen
Ihren Geburtstag keinesfalles übersehen.

Wir gratulieren dieser Frau der lieben
In unserem Namen und der Söhne der sieben.
Dass sie mit ihrem braven Mann
Bald das Friedenfest feiern kann
Eine neue Heimat sich gründen
Das wohlverdiente Glück dort finden
Prag die erste Station wird sein
Wie will ich sie dort fetieren fein
Ihr liebevoll vergelten all die Liebesdienste
Alle zu ersetzen so wie ihre Verdienste.
Wir alle 14 gratulieren alle wünschen
Sie soll nicht den Mut verlieren
Im̄er In Gesundheit gewohnter
Tätigkeit Froh [?] im̄er
Das sind die Wünsche von unserem Zim̄er

Du bist wie eine Blume
So hold so schön so rein
Willst dass ich Dir schreibe
Ein kleines Verselein;
Der Anfang ist wohl richtig
Die Blume hold & zart
Doch spricht der Schluss vom Wehmut
Was nicht nach meiner Art,
Du erwähltest Dir den schönsten
Beruf,
Den Gott nur für begnadete
Menschen schuf

Bist weit über Magdeburgs
Grenzen bekannt
Und nur die blonde schöne Ärztin
genannt,
Ich wünsche Dir nach Prag
baldige Rückkehr
Und so viel Schönes noch mehr
Eine Praxis gross & einträglich

[*Birthday poem*]

Mrs. Heiman, we would in no way overlook your
birthday:

We congratulate a dear lady, this once
In our name and our seven sons
That soon with her man, her good helping mate
The coming of peace she will celebrate
(5)   To build a new home she will begin
Well-earned good fortune she will win
Prague will be her trip's first station
There I would hold a celebration
Reward her kind acts with love and grace
(10) Repay all she earned and her losses replace.
We fourteen congratulate you again
At all times you should your courage retain
In health and activity may you bloom
These are the wishes of our room

Du bist wie eine Blume
So hold, so schön, so rein
Willst dass ich Dir schreibe
Ein kleines Verselein.
Der Anfang ist wohl richtig
Die Blume hold und zart
Doch spricht der Schluss von Wehmut
Was nicht nach meiner Art
Du erwähltest Dir den schönsten Beruf
Den Gott nur für begnadete Menschen schuf
Bist weit über Magdeburgs Grenzen bekannt
Und nur die schöne blonde Ärztin genannt
Ich wünsch Dir nach Prag baldige Rücker

Und so viel Schönes noch mehr
Eine Praxis gross und einträglich
Und allseitige grosse Verehrung
In Liebe und in klingender Währung
Ich selbst werde mich woh nicht davon
     überzeugen
Denn ich fürchte Theresienstadt macht mich zu
     Eigen.

[To a doctor]

You are just like a flower
So fair, so pure, so bright
The little verse you asked for
I willingly here write.
(5)   It starts just as it ought to
The flower fair and fine
But ends in notes of sorrow
Which hasn't been my line.
The profession you chose is one of the best
(10) God only bestowed it on those that He blessed
Your fame far from Magdeburg's borders has flown
You are as the blond pretty doctor now known
I wish that to Prague you soon will return
And all the good things in life there will earn
(15) A practice rich with remuneration
From everyone appreciation
In tinkle of cash and veneration
Too bad that I cannot share this belief
I fear that in Terezín I'll come to grief.

TRANSLATOR'S NOTES

"The professor's wife . . ." line 2
Cherusker: Probably the nickname of someone who shared the lady's last name. The Cheruskers were a German tribe that fought the Romans in Caesar's time.

"The professor's wife . . ." line 4
makes noodles (literally, "makes noodles without pattern"): Though underfed to the point of constant hunger, by pooling food and inventing means of preparing it, women in Terezín managed to do a small amount of cooking. Mina Pächter may also be referring here only to recipes collected from her hungry roommates.

"The professor's wife . . ." line 9
daily proclamations: The orders of the day, posted by the Germans. The "chits" announced the distribution of food, for example, the camp's thin soup.

"January 1943, Theresienstadt," line 5
Ubikation: Dormitory.

"January 1943, Theresienstadt," line 25
from the East: From Auschwitz. Mina originally wrote: "alles Besser als gehn nach dem Osten" (anything is better than going to the East), then crossed it out.

"January 1943, Theresienstadt," line 55
Xantipe: Xanthippa. The wife of Socrates, said to have been a shrew.

"January 1943, Theresienstadt," line 74
These lines are unclear. "*Honeymoon*" may imply that the niece was newly arrived at Terezín.

"Birthday poem," line 9
Mina Pächter may have been unhappy with this rhyme, because she wrote next to it "doesn't go."

"To a doctor," line 11
Magdeburg: The large brick barracks of Terezín had names, and one (perhaps where the doctor worked) was named after the German city of Magdeburg.

EDITOR'S NOTES

"The professor's wife . . ." line 2
Mina Pächter may have been using the Cheruskers symbolically, suggests Dina Abramowicz of YIVO, because ultimately they were absorbed by the Saxons and became extinct.

"January 1943, Theresienstadt," line 13
Although the Nazis dictated the number of people who were to be called for each transport to the East, they craftily left the soul-destroying choice of which individuals actually filled the quota to the Jewish Council of Elders. As a result, *protekce*, which was primarily a way of avoiding the dreaded transports by being under the protection of an important individual or sometimes by having an important job, became a way of life in Terezín.

"January 1943, Theresienstadt," lines 33–37
Because of grave problems with infectious diseases in Theresienstadt, it was considered extremely important to keep the

toilets clean. To make sure hygienic standards were maintained, someone was always on duty in the latrines.

"To a doctor," line 11
Magdeburg was the "town hall" of Terezín and functioned primarily, though not entirely, as an office building for the Council of Jewish Elders and others.

Meine geliebten Geschwister
Unendlich habe ich mich
mit Eurer lieben Karte
gefreut Gottlob dass Ihr
gesund + beisammen seid.
Unsere Nichte konnte nicht
sprechen da sie abgereist ist.
Ich danke Euch für die
Muster ohne Wert Sendung
mit Einbrenn die Ihr
mir von Pressburg
sandtet + das mich sehr
freute. Ich bin gesund
wiege wieder meine 51
Kilo + sehe gut aus
Habt keine Sorgen über
Euern Sohn, der ist ein
kluger zielbewusster Mensch
Ich grüsse Euch in Liebe +
alle l verwandten + bin eue

LETTERS

BY
WILHELMINA (MINA) PÄCHTER

Written in Terezín

Meine geliebten Geschwister
  *Unendlich habe ich mich mit Euerer lieben Karte gefreut. Gottlob
dass Ihr gesund und beisamen seid. Unsere Nichte konnte [ich] nicht
sprechen da sie abgereist ist. Ich danke Euch für die Muster ohne Wert
Sendung mit Einbrenn die Ihr mir von Pressburg sandtet und die mich
sehr freute. Ich bin gesund und wiege wieder meine 51 Kilo und sehe
gut aus. Habt keine Sorgen über Euren Sohn, der ist ein kluger,
zielbewusster Mensch. Ich küsse Euch in Liebe alle Verwandten und
bin Eure*

Mina

My dear sisters
  Your card has brought me endless joy. Thank God you are
healthy and together. Our niece could not say anything since
she has left us. I thank you for sending to me Einbrenn [a
browned roux] from Pressburg [Bratislava] by sample without
value [cheap package mail] which brought me great joy. I am
healthy and again weigh my 51 kilos and look very good. Have
no worry about your son, he is a clever and goal-oriented person. I kiss you in love, all (my) relatives, am yours

Mina

Meine Geliebten

Ich kann Euch unmöglich die grosse Freude schildern, die wir, und inbesondere ich hatte, als Peterls Brief kam. Erinnert ihn nur oft an mich, damit er nicht an mich vergisst. Wir möchten gerne mehr über Euch wissen wollen, aber ich bin schon zufrieden wenn ich weiss dass Ihr gesund seid und dass Ihr Euer Auskommen habt, ich weiss zwar nicht die Art Euerer Beschäftigung. Es ist mir nur leid dass Du Annerl so mager geworden bist. Seit einem Jahr waren die wenige Worte Deiner Daranschrift an Berts Brief das erste Lebenszeichen. Kannst Du denn Heinz, wenn Du ihn siehst, nicht veranlassen, mir einen Gruss zu schreiben?

Mein Leben ist nicht gerade ganz leicht und ich ertrage alles gerne in der Hoffnung Euch wiederzusehen. Die Eltern kommen täglich zu mir, ich gehe den ganzen Winter nicht heraus. Ich küsse Euch vielemals, grüsse die Sterns, Eure

Mutter

My beloved

It is impossible to convey our great joy and especially mine at the arrival of little Peter's letter. Just remind him often of me so that he does not forget me. We would like to know more about you but I am satisfied when I know you are healthy and all your needs are met, though I do not know your occupation. I am just sorry that you, little Anny, have become so thin. The few words you added to Bert's letter were the first sign of life in the past year. Couldn't you ask Heinz, when you see him, to write me a greeting?

My life right now is not easy and I suffer everything willingly in the hope of seeing you again. The parents come daily to me, but all winter I have not stepped outside. I kiss you many times, greet the Sterns, your

Mother

Můj milej zlatej Petřičku!
Já tobě nemohu vyslovět jak jsem se já s Tvoj psaním těšila, ja ho
několikráte četla aš ho umím naspamět. Těšim se velice že jse tě vede
dobře a že jsi zdráv.
Take babička Otti a dědoušek Josef si velice s tvém psani těšili. Prosim
Petřičku jen mně zase brzy piš. Kurty tě též nechá pozdravovati, čti
někdy také česky abychom si tu krasnou řeč nezapoměl[i].
Na mém noční stolku mám tvoji práci vynáles ty malé letadla ležet
a těším [se] a obdivuji vždy tvoji píli a práci. Ja ti brzy navštivim jen
Petřičku prosim tě nazapomen na baby, tak rád ti žadný jiny nemá.
Zde jest veliká zíma a mnoho sněhu a ja si vsopemenu jak ty jsi dělal
toho sněhového panáka. Že ti těsi ta elekrická dráha, jest mě milé,
kdybych mohla já bych ti poslala různé hračky. Ze jiš také na poli
pracuješ to jest krásný. Já jsi každý večer tvuj obrázek libám a prosim
Pana Boha aby tě ještě mohla obejmout. Jen prosim tě Petřičku
nezapomen na mě. Ja ti mnoho a mnohokrate líbám a jes jen hodně
aby jsi byl silný.

Tisic pusinek ti posilá Tvoje babi

[Translated from the Czech]
My dear golden Petřičku [Little Peter]!

I can't express how happy I was with your letter. I read it a
number of times and I know it now by heart. I am delighted that
you are doing well and that you are healthy.

Also, grandma Otti and grandpa Josef were delighted with
your writing. Please Petřičku write again soon. Kurti also sends
his regards. Read also sometimes in Czech so that we do not
forget this beautiful language.

I have on my night table your work and invention, the little
planes. I always admire your work and diligence. I will visit you
soon, only Petřičku, please do not forget babi. Nobody loves

you as much as I do. It is very cold here and a lot of snow and I remember how you made the snowman. I am delighted that the electric train pleases you. If I could I would send you different toys. That you also work in the fields is wonderful. Every evening I kiss your picture and I beg God to let me embrace you again. Only please, Petřičku, do not forget me. I kiss you many, many times and eat a lot to be strong.

Thousand kisses sends you, your, babi

Translator's Notes

"My dear sisters"
It is not known to whom this letter was addressed. Mina Pächter had five sisters, but it is uncertain if any of them were alive at the time. Roux is a mixture of flour and fat, used in cooking.

"My beloved . . ."
Addressed to Anny. Anny and Heinz were Mina's daughter and son, living in Palestine. "The parents" were those of Anny's husband George, and Bert was George's brother.

"My beloved golden Petřičku"
Peter was Mina Pächter's grandson, the son of Anny and George Stern, and was about 10 years old at the time. He was renamed David in Israel. Ottilia and Josef were George's parents, and Kurti Koralek was one of Peter's playmates, a neighbor in his home-town and a distant relative.

Editor's Notes

"My dear sisters"
Those who had einbrenn, a browned roux, were considered for-tunate. It could be added to soup to make it more nutritious or,

says Brown, whose family packed a jar of it to bring to Terezín with them, it could be spread on bread and topped with sugar. It could also be eaten with a spoon.

"My beloved golden Petřičku"
Mina Pächter was a native German speaker from the Sudeten, whose command of written Czech appears to have been limited (see original).

WILHELMINA PÄCHTER
A BIOGRAPHICAL SKETCH
BY DAVID STERN

Wilhelmina ("Mina") Pächter was born 16 July 1872 in Hluboka (Frauenberg) in southern Bohemia, sixth and youngest daughter of Heinrich Stein, a tanner. On the steep hill above Hluboka stands a famous castle, still a tourist attraction, where the Counts of Schwarzenberg lived, formerly Bohemia's most powerful family. Mina's greatgrandfather Wolf (Ze'ev) Lazar Stein (1700–62?) was already a tanner and also a "Hofjude," court Jew to the Count of Schwarzenberg.

At the time Mina was growing up, few women were accepted at universities, and she therefore attended a teachers' seminary in Prague, studying art and literature. (In her later years she always kept by her bedside a copy of Goethe's "Faust," which she often quoted, as well as Shakespeare's "King Lear" and a Hebrew prayer book bound in silver with her own monogram—usually along with a recent crime novel.)

About 1900 she married Adolf Pächter, to the dismay of the elder Steins—for Adolf was a widower with six children, who was twenty-seven years older than his bride. In 1904 her son Heinz (Hanoch) arrived, and three years later a daughter, Anna Wilma. Adolf had six other children from previous marriages, some grown, others young; Mina became mother for all of them.

The family led a prosperous existence, occupying several houses in Bodenbach on the steep slope behind Adolf's button factory, the *Schäferwand*, or "shepherds' cliff." About two hundred Jews lived in Bodenbach, and with Adolf's support (he was the wealthiest man in the community) a synagogue was built in 1907. It still exists as a government storehouse.

The family's luck turned in 1915 when Adolf contracted pneumonia and died. He left the factory and his extensive property to his children, expecting them to take care of Mina. But they did not. In time, because none of the children had the skill to run the factory effectively, it passed into other hands.

To support herself, Mina established herself as an art dealer. She had excellent social connections and was sometimes called into court as an expert witness. She also accumulated an impressive art collection of her own, later looted by the Nazis. Her daughter Anny followed her lead and studied art history.

In 1930 Anny married George Stern, an attorney from Lovosice (Lobositz), another river town about thirty miles upstream. Not long afterwards, Mina came to live with her daughter and with her grandson Peter (later called David).

It was a happy arrangement, but happiness did not last. Hitler rose to power and Jewish refugees began arriving in Bodenbach. Unfortunately, most residents of the Czech borderland were Germans and many openly supported Hitler.

The Czech republic resisted the Nazis until the infamous Munich Pact of September 1938, when its French and British allies agreed not to intervene if Germany overran the Czech borderland. Soon the German army marched in, swastika flags appeared all over the town, and all Jews had to flee.

Anny Stern grabbed her suitcase and boarded a train for Prague; George was with the Czech army, called up (before the British and French caved in) to resist a Nazi invasion, and later he joined her. Mina arrived by one of the last trains, and all other members of the Pächter and Stern families also fled. In March 1939, however, the Nazis occupied the rest of the country.

George Stern, Anny's husband, escaped to Palestine. Anny Stern became involved in Jewish emigration to Palestine, securing visas and funds for Jewish refugees as an official of the "Palestine Office" supervised by Adolf Eichmann, a leader of anti-Jewish persecutions. At the end of November 1939, by great luck and thanks to the steadfast support of community leader Jakob (Yankev) Edelstein, she and her son were allowed to leave for Palestine.

Of the family members that stayed behind, only one survived: Liesel (Elizabeth), granddaughter of Adele Hirsch, Adolf Pächter's second wife. She was in eleventh grade when the Nazis invaded; and, when all Jews were expelled from public schools, she volunteered to be trained as a nurse, later working in Jewish hospitals and marrying one of the doctors, Dr. Ernest Reich.

In 1942 most of Prague's Jews were transferred to the old fortress town of Terezín (Theresienstadt), into which ultimately all Czech Jews were crammed. For many of them, including Liesel's parents and sister, that was only a brief stop before a final trip to Auschwitz and destruction. Liesel and her husband left Prague for Terezín in March 1943.

Liesel had been working for four or five months at the ghetto hospital when she heard that Mina Pächter was there. By the time she found her, Mina was in poor health. Residents of Terezín were always hungry and often starving, food rations were meager, and many came down with "hunger edema," which we now know signified protein deficiency. For older people, that was the beginning of the end.

Liesel arranged for Mina to be brought to the hospital and tended her as well as she could. Mina stayed mostly in bed, gradually getting weaker. She died on Yom Kippur, 1944, when much of Terezín's original population was already gone. Liesel watched as her body was taken to the crematorium outside the walls, the final destination for thousands of Jews.

BIBLIOGRAPHY

Auerbacher, Inge. *I Am a Star, Child of the Holocaust*. New York: Puffin Books, 1993.

Beltrone, Art and Lee. *A Wartime Log*. Charlottesville: Howell Press, 1995.

Berenbaum, Michael. *The World Must Know*. Boston & New York: Little, Brown and Company, 1993.

Berkley, George. *Hitler's Gift, the Story of Theresienstadt*. Boston: Branden Books, 1993.

Bondy, Ruth. *"Elder of the Jews," Jakob Edelstein of Theresienstadt*. New York: Grove Press, 1989.

Bridenthal, Renate, et al., ed. *When Biology Becomes Destiny*. New York: New Feminist Library, 1984.

Fowler, Colonel H. C. *Recipes out of Bilibid*. New York: George W. Stewart, 1946.

Friedman, Saul S., ed. *The Terezín Diary of Gonda Redlich*. Lexington: The University Press of Kentucky, 1992.

Green, Gerald. *The Artists of Terezin*. New York: Hawthorn Books, 1978.

Gutman, Israel, ed. *Encyclopedia of the Holocaust*. New York: Macmillan Publishing, 1990.

Hess, O. and A. *Viennese Cooking*. New York: Crown, 1957.

Hilberg, Raul. *The Destruction of the European Jews*. New York: Holmes & Meier, 1985.

Kaplan, Marion A. "Jewish Women in Nazi Germany." *Feminist Studies* 16:3 (Fall 1990), 579–606.

Kirshenblatt-Gimblett, Barbara. "Kitchen Judaism." In *Getting Comfortable in New York, the American Jewish Home, 1880–1950*, ed. Susan L. Braunstein and Jenna Weissman

Joselit, pp. 75–105). New York: The Jewish Museum, 1990.

Krejčová, Helena. "State Your Views on Assimilation and Anti-Semitism." *Review of the Society for the History of Czechoslovak Jews* VI: 15–26.

Lagus, Karel, et al. *Terezín*. Prague: Council of Jewish Communities of the Czech Lands, 1965.

Lang, George. *The Cuisine of Hungary*. New York: Atheneum, 1971.

Langer, Lawrence L., ed. *Art from the Ashes*. New York: Oxford, 1994.

Lederer, Zdenek. *Ghetto Theresienstadt*. New York: Howard Fertig, 1983.

Lustig, Arno, et al. *Seeing through "paradise."* Boston: Massachusetts College of Art, 1991.

Petrášová, Markéta. "Art in the Concentration Camp of Terezin." *Judaica Bohemiae* XXI: 50–61.

Salomon, Gertrud. "Barley, barley" (from the Elsa Oestreicher Collection, Leo Baeck Institute). *LBI News* 50 (Summer 1985), p. 5.

Schwertfeger, Ruth. *Women of Theresienstadt*. Oxford & New York: Berg, 1989.

Troller, Norbert. *Theresienstadt, Hitler's Gift to the Jews*. Chapel Hill & London: University of North Carolina Press, 1991.

Volavková, Hana, ed. . . . *I never saw another butterfly* . . . New York: Schocken Books, 1993.

Wechsberg, Joseph. *Blue Trout & Black Truffles*. New York: Knopf, 1966.

———. *The Cooking of Vienna's Empire*. New York: Time-Life, 1968.

West, Richard. "The Vertical Village." *New York Magazine* (March 23, 1981), pp. 23–26.

Cara De Silva is an award-winning journalist who specializes in ethnicity. She was a feature writer for *Newsday/New York Newsday*, where her beat was ethnic New York and where her food- and- culture column, "Flavor of the Neighborhood," ran for six years. Her articles have also appeared in the *New York Times*; the *Washington Post*; *Food & Wine*; *Eating Well*; *Cuisine*; and *Diversion* magazines. As an editor, De Silva has worked on cookbook series, novels, and scholarly books, and as a teacher she has taught courses in food and culture at the City University. A featured speaker at conferences and seminars, she has also appeared as a guest on local and national television and radio shows. Currently, she is writing a novel and working on a book about subcultures in America.

Bianca Steiner Brown, a native of Prague, was deported to the ghetto/concentration camp of Terezín in September 1942. While there, she worked primarily as a nurse. After liberation in May 1945, she returned to Prague but left with her family following the Communist takeover in 1948, moving first to Ecuador and then, in 1951, to the United States. A deeply knowledgeable cook with a broad general interest in food, she has worked as an associate food editor for both *Good House-keeping* magazine and *Gourmet* magazine and has also been a consultant for Weight Watchers cookbooks. Now retired, she teaches popular adult-education cooking classes on Long Island.

Michael Berenbaum is director of the United States Holocaust Research Institute of the U.S. Holocaust Memorial Museum and the Hymen Goldman adjunct professor of theology at Georgetown University in Washington, D.C. A social thinker who has authored scores of scholarly articles, hundreds of journalistic pieces, and ten books—among them *The World Must Know: The History of the Holocaust As Told in the United States Holocaust*

Memorial Museum—he is recognized for combining his writing talents with political activism. In 1995, he coproduced "One Survivor Remembers: The Gerda Weissman Klein Story" with Home Box Office, which won an Oscar for best short documentary and earned Berenbaum both an Emmy Award and a CableAce Television Award. He holds a doctorate from Florida State University and has been awarded numerous fellowships, among them the Danforth Fellowship and the George Wise Fellow at Tel Aviv University.

David Peter Stern, Mina Pächter's grandson, was born in Bodenbach, Czechoslovakia, in 1931. When the Germans invaded in 1938, his family fled to Prague, from which, late in 1939, he and his mother escaped to British Palestine to join his father, George. After earning his doctorate in Israel for the study of cosmic rays, Stern moved to the United States where since 1961 he has worked as a physicist at NASA's Goddard Space Flight Center in Greenbelt, Maryland. The author of many papers on physics and the history of space research, his *Exploration of the Earth's Magnetosphere* can be found on the Worldwide Web.